Me Versus Me

THE STRUGGLE TO BE YOUR BETTER SELF

Milola Charles

ISBN 978-1-63874-678-2 (paperback)
ISBN 978-1-63874-679-9 (digital)

Christian Faith Publishing, Inc.
832 Park Avenue
Meadville, PA 16335
www.christianfaithpublishing.com

Printed in the United States of America

Dedication

I want to thank my Lord and Savior Jesus Christ who gave me the strength and vision to write and complete this book. I thank God for using my voice and experiences as an instrument to be a blessing to others.

To the queen of my heart, my mother:

> You saw me as an author before I saw it happened. You pushed and molded me into the woman I am today. Thank you, Mom, for being my mother and my friend. Thank you for anchoring me with your love and endless prayers. Thank you for allowing me to be the person God has called me to be and for your help in pushing me toward my purpose.

To my dad:

> Our journey has not always been perfect, but I am thankful for where we are today. I appreciate the unconditional love that you have for me.

To my siblings and my niece—Lolami, Lolayemi, and Milanae:

> You inspire me every day, and I love you so much. Thank you for pushing me and motivating me.

To my big brother in heaven, Milade:

> I believed in myself and made it happen with God. I know you are proud. I love you forever!

To all my dear friends who supported me throughout this process, you are appreciated.

Contents

Introduction...7

1 The Sunken Place 11

Heartbreak Motel 11

Rejection 25

Loss 35

2 Living Under Sexual Thoughts (LUST) 49

Celibacy while Single...56

Celibacy in a Relationship 61

3 Daddy Issues...69

4 Hello, Fear..77

5 Friendships 89

The Power of Friendships 89

Like-Minded People 91

Comparison Is a Killer...93

6 New Beginnings 100

Introduction

Have you ever struggled with becoming the best version yourself? Have you ever felt like your heart is telling you one thing, but your mind is telling you another? Have you ever battled against your fleshly desire versus what God wants you to do? I'm sure most of you have. That's why this book is called *Me Versus Me*. You, the one who wants to do the right thing, versus the you who just can't get it right. The one who wants to practice celibacy versus the one who enjoys foreplay and sex. The one who no longer wants to masturbate and watch porn versus the one who does it routinely. Is this you?

I'm sure some of you may have heard the motto "The heart wants what the heart wants." Why is that though? As human beings, how do we know what our heart wants? In the Bible, it says that the heart is very deceiving. So if we compare "The heart wants what the heart wants" to what the scripture says, then the real question would be if the heart is a good measuring tool to determine how much you should trust someone. You may have also heard the saying, "Follow your heart. Let it guide you." The truth is, if you don't know the condition of your heart, then you can't trust it enough to lead you to the right decision. My question is, what is the condition of your heart? What does your heart look like? The Bible says, "Out of the heart, the mouth speaks." Everything you say is really coming from your heart. This is why when people say things in anger, they often take it back and apologize. Even if the apology sometimes softens the blow, it still doesn't change whatever was said. You have a heart issue. We all do. Let's talk about it

This book is for those who are in Christ but are constantly struggling to be better. To get ultimate freedom in whatever area you are struggling with, you have got to have a heart check, which means to examine all the areas of your life and your heart and to determine why you do what you do and see if those things glorify God. They say insanity is defined by doing something over and over again and expecting you will get a different result. If you truly want to be free, you have to acknowledge first that the secret sin you love is something God hates. That is the first step to becoming free from yourself. The ultimate goal is to get to the point where you begin to hate your secret sins as much as God does. Please understand that it's not an easy process, and you definitely cannot do it alone. You have to have a heart check to examine what the content of your heart looks like.

There are so many Christians who are struggling in some area of sin with no one to talk to. I wrote this book to shed light on those things and create a platform that can be a start to your freedom. However, it will only work if you are serious about God and being saved. There are so many people who feel judged when they do something wrong and don't know to pray because they think God is mad at them. Sometimes they may feel dirty on the inside and don't know how to pray or seek God's help. The content in this book will help you navigate through that. God loves you, but He hates sin. Do not be a hypocrite and continue to read this book if you are not willing to do the work. The tools in this book are not a magic trick or something you can use as a cover-up while living in sin. I need you to understand that your heart is the issue here. You can still win because God has already won all your battles, but the choice is still up to you. If you are reading this book, I want you to know that there is no judgment or condemnation to you. I want you to know that even in your worst situation, God sees you as you are. God sees if you are hurting, sees what you need, and sees your heart. Regardless of what you are or have been through, you can still be free.

The problem is, a lot of people preach more about religion than relationships. I want you to think of it as this. When a man first meets a woman he is interested in, or vice versa, in order for both parties to really enjoy one another, there has to be some form of effort from both parties. In order for a woman or a man to really get close to the person they are dating, they have to take their time to get to know them, right? They have to talk to each other and spend time with each other. Well, that's how building a relationship with God is. You have to spend time talking to Him and listening to Him to get to know Him. How can you say you know Him if you haven't taken your time with Him? How can you say you know someone unless you make an effort to get to know them? How can you say you like or not like something unless you experienced it? A relationship with Jesus is the same way. You have to be committed, be open, and willing to learn and grow. I have nothing against the church itself. I believe that the church should be seen as a hospital for the sick. I practice having a relationship, not religion.

For instance, you can take someone who lived in poverty their whole lives into a wealthy suburban community, but if you do not change the mindset of this person, they will continue to exhibit things and act in their old way of thinking. Becoming a Christian and accepting Christ into your life is the same way. You can join a church, be baptized, and turn away from your old ways. God will forgive and forget all your habits and sins. However, it is still up to you to adopt and put into practice a new way of thinking to fit your new way of lifestyle. If you read this book until the end, then two things will happen: your life will either remain in the same state as it was before you started reading or it will be transformed into something better. Your choice!

1

The Sunken Place

Heartbreak Motel

I was watching a movie called *Get Out*, directed by Jordan Peele, a movie that deals with issues of racism and white supremacy. In one of the scenes, the main character is hypnotized and sent into a fugue state of consciousness called the Sunken Place. The movie described it as a very scary dark place with no escape, a place of no freedom, a place of hopelessness that was impossible to get out of. Even though it was just a movie, I started to compare the Sunken Place to real-life circumstances. There are so many broad topics that could relate to it, but I felt passionate about three things that can cause you and me to get into a similar place, such as heartbreak, rejection, and loss.

Heartbreak is something that everyone had at some point and can relate to. It is the only pain that cannot be felt physically but emotionally. The art of this trauma varies from person to person, depending on the situation, but everyone has experienced heartbreak at some point in their lives. If you haven't, I pray that you never will. However, it's so important to understand how to deal with and handle this pain because how you choose to handle your heartbreak is so crucial to your breakthrough and freedom.

I am the type of woman that immerses herself in every serious relationship or commitment. Before I agree to be committed to anyone, there are few things that I am looking for. Being a God-fearing man is the top of the list. Followed by someone who values quality time, like-minded, someone who is funny and is family oriented. Simple enough! I dated a guy, let's call him Justin. When we first met, I thought he was very attractive. Justin seemed to have a great relationship with God, and we had great chemistry...or so I thought! I was sold on Justin's make-believe passion for the Lord and his willingness to serve as well as how he treated me. Fast-forward to several months into our relationship, Justin got sick. He had melanoma cancer and a brain tumor that triggered multiple seizures. This was a lot for me to deal with as a partner, but I knew that he needed me to stick by his side. Being the type of woman that I am, I decided to stick it out with him because there was no way I was going to let my man go through this himself. So I was missing work, going to hospitals, and making sure he was well taken care of. After all was said and done, I still felt unappreciated and unvalued.

Justin had children. I knew that going into the relationship. I also knew that because he has kids, I will never be a top priority. I was okay with that in the beginning. What I wanted—rather, what I felt I deserved was to feel valued. I believe every man or woman would like to feel important and valued in their relationship at any given time, whether their significant other has kids or not. As Justin's illness became worse, his priorities in our relationship changed. He became very nonchalant and didn't want to live. He didn't care anymore about our relationship or himself. It saddened me to think that the man that I love so dearly didn't love himself enough to fight to live. We eventually became distant. Daily conversations became weekly, text messages became fewer, and quality time become practically nonexistent.

I was always an independent woman. I knew my worth. Deep down, I wasn't happy, but I loved this man so much, and the thought of him not being in my life made me extremely sad. I decided it was time to say good-bye to Justin because I was losing myself. I found myself in the Sunken Place shortly after that. I was missing him! I thought I was committing to a man who couldn't fight his way out of his illness to keep our relationship afloat, but that wasn't all. Before he got sick, they were red flags that I chose to ignore. Those red flags started to show increasingly after he becomes sick. He was always angry and snapped at me all the time. He was very controlling. He didn't want me to go out unless he came with me and didn't want me making or having friends. He generally just wanted to control my life. This man also had a past that he kept hidden from me for a while. There were some anger issues and insecurities that I noticed. This man abused me verbally but told me I was his queen in the same breath. I was the same one who held him down when he was in need even after he got sick. After everything he put me through, was I still supposed to be with him on account that he was sick? Did I deserve to be treated like my opinions didn't matter or feel neglected?

Let me just be clear, everything that happened between Justin and I wasn't all bad. I am not one to bash my ex, but I'm just stating some facts as to why I chose to leave. My first mistake in this relationship was that I gave my all to a man who didn't understand what a commitment was and wasn't led by God. I gave my heart to a man I thought had the attributes of a good leader, only to realize he couldn't even lead himself. God made man in His image (men and women). He also made man the head of the household, made woman out of man, and made her be submissive to a man. I know there are a lot of women who hear the word *submissive* and cringe, and I can understand why. The problem is, there are men who want women to submit to them but aren't willing to be a proper leader. "But I want you to understand that the head of every man is Christ, the head of a woman is a man, and the head of Christ is God" (1 Corinthians 11:3). Submit to each other. Now some men take these words very negatively and use that as an excuse to mistreat their wives. The truth is, at the end of the day, a good woman will have no problem submitting to a good man who is worthy of her submission. What God is saying is that since He made man in His image, a man is automatically under God's authority and under His cover. Since God made woman out of a man, then she should be under his covering and protection because they both come from God. This is the structure that God was referring to in a man being a leader.

AS A WOMAN, IF YOU WANT A MAN TO LEAD YOU, IT IS YOUR DUTY TO FIND OUT WHOSE PROTECTION OR COVERING THIS MAN IS UNDER

Therefore, as a woman, if you want a man to lead you, it is your duty to find out whose protection or covering this man is under. Who does he use as his protection? Is it God? Is it self? Is it money? Is it ambition? For a man to truly lead you on the right path, he has to be *solely* led by God and strictly under His authority. If he is, then he can lead you correctly. In God's eyes, the woman is as important to the man as the man is important to the woman because they both come from Him. Remember that if a man is truly under God's authority, his action will show it, and he will treat you right.

BEFORE YOU GET INTO ANY RELATIONSHIP, YOU HAVE TO LEARN HOW TO BE WHOLE

Never forget who you are in a relationship. Never get so engulfed in a relationship that you start to lose track of who you are. Before you get into any relationship, you have to learn how to be whole and unique with your individual self because you aren't just attaching yourself to that person, but you are bringing yourself as an individual. That's the only way it's going to work. I wish I knew then what I know now because when I was with Justin, I completely lost who I was. I was doing things I normally would not do. I found myself picking up habits and "soul ties." We will talk more about this in my next book, *The Person on the Other Side of the Bed.*

I decided that enough was enough. I needed to take a step back. I needed to take a break to regain composure and reanalyze who I was, my likes and dislikes, etc. I needed to take time and figure it all out. I realized that when you have been with someone for such a long time, you build a strong bond, which makes it hard sometimes to leave the person. If it's not right, you will definitely know it. If you aren't happy, then find happiness, even if that happiness involves you being by yourself for a while. I used to say this quote all the time, "I will rather be by myself, alone, and be happy than to be with someone and feel miserable." So I left!

My next story is about another ex. Let's call him Patrick. Now I met Patrick about a year after I left Justin. I was in a good place in my life. My relationship with God was blossoming. I was also in good mental space, and I was happy. Patrick was perfect to me…or so I thought. Patrick almost had everything I wanted in a husband, except for a relationship with God. This was a red flag for me, but I decided to not take heed and proceeded anyway. I am a hopeless romantic, however, it takes a lot for me to actually fall for a guy. After Justin and I broke up, I didn't date seriously for about a year and a half. Then I met Patrick. We had so much in common, and our families knew each other. I just knew that he was the one for me.

One thing that I can say about me is that in all of my relationships, marriage has always been the end goal. I suppose that's why I took my commitments seriously. There were so many pros to Patrick that I overlooked the cons. I overlooked the little things that grew into big things. Patrick was so good with his words. He told me exactly what I wanted to hear. He gave me enough for me to think that he loved me and cared about me, and I honestly believed him.

There is a famous proverb that says, "What is done in the dark will always come to the light." When someone says that they love you, remember that they need to show you. Love requires action and sacrifice. If someone is *truly* for you, then they will show those qualities. I personally do not believe there is a timeline to fall in love. They say that it takes a lifetime to truly get to know someone so, technically, there is no actual timeline to say you love someone. However, what I have learned as an adult is that loving someone should be unconditional. Ladies, if a guy ever tells you that he loves you and tells you why, run! He only loves you for what you can do for him or what you have done for him. Be cautious because if you stop doing these "conditional things," his feelings might change.

Anyway, things went pretty fast for Patrick and me. He told me he loved me first, and I believed him. We talked about marriage, a wedding, having kids, and building a life together as a couple. I urge you not to be swayed by words but watch their actions, as it will reveal their true character. One day, Patrick and I were spending time

15

together in my place when he suggested that he wanted to meet my family. After Justin, I didn't bring anyone home to meet my parents. When it comes to my family, I am very territorial and protective, so I don't just bring just anyone home, especially because things didn't exactly work out between Justin and me. When Patrick suggested meeting my parents, I was nervous but also excited. When the day came, I got a phone call from him a few hours before the dinner party. He said that he had a "family emergency" and that he is just not sure how long that will last. I was perplexed! "Today of all days, you have a family emergency?" He was like, "Yes, babe, but I will call you and let you know how things go."

For some reason, I knew he was lying. Women have this thing called intuition. If we feel something isn't right, it's probably because it isn't. Sometimes we tend to ignore this feeling because of love. Granted, I understand that things happen in life that are completely out of your control, but what makes a difference is how you handle those surprising situations when they do happen. I waited and waited to see if he was going to call, but he never did. I waited for a few hours, and the dust started to settle. I called him and left him a message. I didn't get a call back. All of a sudden, I started to see things clearly. I began to realize that maybe he didn't care enough about the relationship as much as I did. I was always cautious about dating. I made my interest known enough but not too much that I felt vulnerable. His action pretty much showed that he was a coward who couldn't be transparent and honest about how he truly felt.

After this happened, I doubted myself. I started to think that maybe it was me. *Did I do something wrong? Did I say something wrong? Did I come off too strong? God, why did You let this happen to me? Was it because of sex? How could You see me go through this and do nothing?*

Celibacy in a relationship is very difficult. If the guy you're dating doesn't understand why you are practicing celibacy, then it's not going to work, regardless of how good you are to him in the relationship. If you are dating someone you think is the right one for you, pray about it before jumping into it. Understand that God will not bless a mess!

IF YOU GET INTO A RELATIONSHIP THAT GOD DIDN'T PUT TOGETHER, YOU CANNOT EXPECT GOD TO BLESS IT

If you get into a relationship that God didn't put together, you cannot expect God to bless it. I have seen cases where people would get into a relationship and start praying to God in an attempt to change the other person into who they would like them to be. You can't get into a relationship without permission from God. In your prayer, ask God to bless it. Don't say, "God, change him or her" or "If only You could just open their eyes to see that I'm the right one for them..." But the problem is that you cannot tell God to bless a union that He didn't put together.

As women, when we meet a guy that we like or perhaps feel like he is husband material, we don't take our time to form a friendship with this person first. It's so important to establish a foundation of friendship first before anything else. To be clear, being friends first doesn't mean that you put that person in the friend zone, unless those are your intentions. It means that you talk and establish a foundation with the intention of growing into something, like being friends with a purpose. When you meet someone that you are interested in, most people subconsciously look for things in people that they are lacking in themselves. For example, if you are someone who didn't have a father or mother figure growing up, you are subconsciously attracted to a man or woman who exhibits parental characteristics. If you desire an emotional connection, you subconsciously cling to your significant other. Similarly, if you have low self-esteem, you will subconsciously cling to someone who is much more confident than you.

Now this attraction to someone with the opposite personality isn't necessarily a bad thing in a healthy relationship because the reality is that your spouse or your partner is supposed to compliment you. They are supposed to bring out the best version of yourself and uplift you, as you would do for them, despite your differences. However, sometimes seeking a specific characteristic in a significant other can also be counterproductive, depending on the situation. It becomes detrimental only when one party starts to take advantage of the other person by exploiting their vulnerability. An example would in the form of abuse, whether it's physical, verbal, emotional, or mental. An abusive relationship is very unhealthy. I am not an expert so I cannot back up this theory, but I can take a guess that most victims decide to stay in their abusive relationship because of their lack of self-esteem or for their comfort. After being abused for so long, some victims might start to view the abuse as love and have gotten so used to it that they fear getting out of it. There is also mental abuse when they hear things like "No one will ever love you like I do," or "You will never find another person like me," or "You're damaged goods, no one wants you but me."

Another example would be a woman who wasn't the type to be vulnerable. You know, the one who is soft on the inside but puts on an exterior of being "tough," doesn't show any of her weaknesses, and keeps something she is going through to herself because of people who look up to her. Everyone is watching her constantly because she is "strong." What if this woman then meets someone who displays attributes of strength? Perhaps he is a great listener and a great communicator. Perhaps she thinks he gets and understands her, someone who acts like they are patient with her. Sounds familiar? Slowly, her trust builds, and she begins to open up. Her walls start crumbling down. She starts to share things, pouring her heart out to them, only for them to turn against her, prey on her vulnerability and weaknesses, and use the information she shared with them against her.

Please don't get me wrong. I am not saying that everybody that displays these attributes are bad people. What I am saying is that you need to learn to pay attention to someone you are dating. Pay attention to the signs and listen to your intuition, ladies. Understand what self-love is and, most importantly, put God first because once you start to see yourself the way God sees you, and your mind will be completely transformed. The truth is, we human beings all want to love and to be loved because the thought of love and being in love is a beautiful thing. Sometimes we want love so bad, we risk it all for one person. This kind of risk should be done only if you know in your heart and your mind that this person is the one for you. When we meet someone, we don't take the time to ask God what His thoughts are about this person before we jump into a relationship with them. If you are someone who isn't into praying, I strongly suggest that you try it because prayer works. Until then, you are probably the type that chooses not to pay attention to signs both big and small.

I read an article that inspired me written by Sherita Furlow. She wrote that when you meet someone, you have to ask questions (I cannot stress the importance of asking questions) before giving them complete access to your life. Learn not to move so quickly, watch their actions, and let it speak louder than their words, paying attention to the signs just as equally. Sometimes when we meet a potential mate, we automatically just assume God is supposed to bless the relationship by default. Here is a secret, if you are seeking God's guidance on any relationship, His answer is always "no" until he tells you "yes." If you think his answer is yes, please ask for more signs and confirmation. In my next book, *The Person on the Other Side of the Bed* where I talk more about the checklist you should have before getting into a relationship. Unfortunately, I had to learn this lesson the hard way. The bottom line is, before you decide to enter any relationship, seek God's guidance and do not assume God already approves of the person as your partner. Pray about it until you know for a fact that you are supposed to be in that relationship. Until then, there needs to be a red light. God alone knows the heart of man. The Bible has a lot to say about our motives. A motive is the underlying reason for any action. Proverbs 16:2 (NIV) says, "All a person's ways seem pure to them, but motives are weighed by the Lord." Because the human heart is very deceitful (Jeremiah 17:9), we can easily fool ourselves about our own motives. We can pretend that we are choosing certain actions of God for the benefit of others when, in reality, we have selfish reasons. God is not fooled by our selfishness and is "a discerner of the thoughts and intents of the heart" (Hebrews 4:12 NKJV). Human beings operate from a place of selfishness and pride and the only person who can help you decipher who is for you is God.

Heartbreak is something that most people go through. A lot of times, it takes you to this Sunken Place. When I hit rock bottom in both of my relationships, the only direction I could turn to was up. The prayer below helped me a lot in my time of need. Remember that God's love for you is pure and perfect. He loves you more than any human will love you. This is what worked for me. I pray that as you repeat this prayer to yourself, you will be set free from the Sunken Place of heartache in Jesus' name, amen!

Prayer

Put me first and I will give you everything
that you need. (Matthew 6:23)

Lord, Your word says to put You first in everything and You will give me what I need. Lord, teach me and show me how to put You first in all my ways. Teach me how to love and respect You, Lord. Sometimes when it comes to my relationships, I am not always making the right decisions. Sometimes I think only with my heart, my head, or both. Lord I know the journey is not going to be easy, but if You tell me that You will give me everything that I need, including the right relationship, then I choose You today, Lord. I accept You to be the Lord over everything in my life. Today I choose to submit my ways in Your hands, and I ask that You guide my path.

Come to me all who are tired and carrying
heavy loads, and I will give you rest. (Matthew
11:28)

Lord, when it comes to my relationships, I am sick and tired of being sick and tired. Lord, the heartache is unbearable. It hurts so much to the point where I just don't know if I'm going to pull though. Lord, whether this relationship was right for me or not, You said in your word to come to You when I am tired and burdened. Lord, this weight is too heavy for me to carry by myself. This load is too much for me to bear, but I know load that You will give me more than I can handle so I am asking you to give me Your strength to overcome, I give this pain. I give my heart to You. Make me whole again in Jesus' name.

I will heal you of your broken heart and
bandage your wounds. (Psalm 147:3)

When five birds are sold, they may only
cost two pennies. But God does not forget any
of them. Yes, God even knows how many hairs
you have on your head. Do not be afraid. You are
worth much more than birds (Luke 12:6–7).

*Lord, only someone of Your magnitude can know the hairs on my
head, only You can account for that number and show that You love me.
You said, Lord, that You will heal my broken heart and my wounds.
Lord, I have literally given myself foolishly to this person in every area
humanly possible. I gave my time and energy, investing so much that I
know I'll probably not get back. I am hurting, O God! I am broken. Heal
my broken heart, just like You said God. Heal my wounds completely so
I can move on. Your love is so great and perfect that You care about me
way more than the birds in the air. You care about me that You know the
number of hairs of my head. Lord, I thank You for loving me like that.
I just ask that You continue to heal my heart so I can return to a place
of peace.*

I selected you! You belong to me even before
I formed the world. (Ephesians 1:4–5)

In me, you can handle anything. (Philippians
4:13)

*Lord, Your word said that You selected me before You formed the
world. That means that You already knew me before I was born. You
knew what I would be like. You knew what my thoughts would be. You
created me and formed me in your image. Lord, since You know every-
thing and You know who I am, I am asking You to guide me in this
process. Help me, Lord, to become a better person. You said that in You, I
can handle anything. I don't really know how I am truly going to handle
this situation, Lord, but I am asking You to heal me in this process and*

help to get my heart back. I understand that You have my best interest at heart. I also understand that I may not always make the smartest decisions when it comes to my relationships, but, Lord, You are the only one who will never fail me so I trust that You will come through for me in this situation.

Give all your worries to him because he cares for you. (1 Peter 5:7)

Talk to me about your concerns, I will take care of you. You'll be joyful (John 16:24)

Dear God, Your word is telling me to tell You about everything that is bothering me because You care for me. I know my relationship with You isn't perfect, but every day that I wake up means that You have given me another chance and another day to make things perfected by You. Lord, I am hurting with this heartbreak. I really don't know what to do. I don't know how to move forward. I'm asking for Your help. There are so many things going on in my mind mentally. Please get me get through process. I know I'm not where I should be in my work with You, but I thank You, God, because You care about me and will come through for me. Lord, as I am talking to You about my concerns, I ask that You give me that joy You promised In Jesus' name, amen!

Every day I will give you a new strength deep within. (2 Corinthians 4:16–18)

You have nothing to fear because I will carry you through everything. (Isaiah 41:10)

Dear God, You said in Your word that every day You will give a new strength within through my trials. You said that I should fear nothing because You will carry me through everything. Lord, even in this time of need, even in this pain, I am asking You to give me new strength each day as I am going through this. Use this situation to mold me so I will grow.

I honestly don't know how I will make it through this phase in my life by myself, Lord, so here I am asking You for help. In Jesus' name, amen!

When you are praying and you remember that you are angry with another person about something, then forgive him. If you do this, then your Father in heaven will also forgive you. But if you do not forgive those who do you wrong, then your Father in heaven will not forgive your sin. (Mark 11:25–26)

Good news! I will fix your broken heart, and I will set you free. (Isaiah 61:1)

Dear God, in this time of need, I acknowledge that I need Your help, which is why I am here talking to you. Lord, I really need You to help me, but I don't want to pray this prayer in vain, knowing that it won't be answered if I didn't forgive the one who hurt me. I don't know if I can, Lord, but I'm willing to try because I want You to help me. So today, Lord, I forgive_____ for hurting me. I forgive them for using me and manipulating me. I forgive them for abusing me physically, emotionally, or mentally. I forgive them for making me feel like I am worthless. I forgive them for hurting me so much and causing this pain. Most of all, I forgive myself for not seeing my self-worth. I forgive myself for any pain that I have caused them as well. I forgive them, Lord, so You can forgive me off all my sin and so You can hear me when I pray to You. Please fix my broken heart and change the love I have for this person. Please set me free as You promised. In Jesus' name, amen.

I deeply love you and are with you through every trial. (Peter 5:7)

My power is granting you all you need to cope. (2 Peter 2:3)

I, the Lord, am close to the brokenhearted,
and I save those whose spirits have been crushed.
(Psalm 34:18)

Dear heavenly father, I am still learning what it means to love. Maybe I had a misconstrued idea of what true love is. I honestly don't know anymore. What I do know is the fact that Your word say You deeply love me to be there for me through this trial. I welcome that love from You, God. I ask You to fill me up completely with Your love. You said that You are granting me all I need to cope in this situation. I ask for Your strength and power so I can make it through. My heart is broken, Lord, and my spirit has been crushed. Comfort me, Lord, as You are close to those whose hearts have been broken.

According to Wikipedia, love is a variety of different emotional and mental states, typically strongly and positively experienced, that ranges from deepest to interpersonal affection to simple pleasure. It could refer to an emotion or a strong attraction filled with compassion and kindness. However, in the world we live in, love is based on merit, what someone can do for us or what they have done. When we feel like someone loves us, it's usually because of certain acts they have shown. As human being, we are naturally selfish and extremely carnal. We only want to give something to someone when we know we are going to get something in return. We have been taught and trained by society to only show love when it's beneficial for us.

God is love. His love for you isn't merited or conditional. You don't have to do anything more or anything less for Him to love you any more than He already does. You know why? Because He doesn't love You based on your actions. He searches your heart and judges you based on the content of your heart. He loved you so much so that He gave up His only Son to die for your sins and every wrong you have ever done. When you accept Him into your life, He wraps all those stained sins in a bow, forgives you, and never remembers them. Can you ever imagine giving up your only child to die for the sake of another human being? Well, God did! That's how much He loves you. So you see, even when you are heartbroken about a guy or a woman, you have to remember that God is the only person who can give you the unconditional love, which requires you to do nothing but accept Him. Seek God's love first before you seek it from a person. Let his love get you through the Sunken Place of your heartache.

Rejection

If you really think about it, there are a lot of things and issues about our lives that can be linked to rejection. The word *reject* means "to dismiss, to dissatisfy, to deny, to discount, to eliminate, to turn down, to cast out, to refuse, to pass up, to pass by, to shoot down, to exclude, or to throw away." Does any of these words sound familiar to you? There is nothing that hurts more than being rejected, but rest assured that the tools in this chapter will give you more insight on how to overcome. The reality is, the world is filled of people who aren't always going to accept you for whatever reason. There are going to be a lot of open and close doors in your life, and usually happens unexpectedly. There are things that you are going to desire and reject. There are things that you are going to want and won't get. There are going to be times that, regardless of your age and how you look, some people are probably going to reject you.

When I was in my dating for fun, when all I cared about was a free meal, I'd entertain a lot of guys for that purpose. (Yes, fellas! The myth is true). When I met this guy, I didn't think he was the most attractive person in the world. Nonetheless, I entertained him because he seemed like he had a good personality. After we exchanged numbers, we both went our separate ways. At the end of the night, I noticed the same guy was talking to my friend. I didn't really think anything of it because I thought, *Hey! She's my friend. If this guy tries to talk to her as well as me, she would tell me.* He texted me on my way home and said that he had something he wanted to talk to me about. I told him we can talk about it later. He ended up calling me later on that night. I was curious to hear what he wanted to talk to me about. He told me that he would rather go out with my friend. Because my friend spoke the same language as fluently as he did, he thought they would get along better. I remember becoming so upset and feeling instantly insecure. *How could someone not want to talk to me because I didn't speak a language as fluently as he would like?* I was annoyed! I questioned myself. *Was I not pretty enough? Was I not smart enough?* I mean, this guy and I had a conversation literally for an hour when we met, only for him to tell me that I wasn't good enough for him because I didn't speak a language as fluently as he did. I was hurt! I felt rejected and ashamed, especially because nobody ever made me feel like that before. The truth is, rejection stems from insecurities, not knowing who you are or being aware of how powerful your mind is.

As a young Nigerian woman, I have never been the type to be heavily involved in cliques and bought into the hype of social status, but I have always loved people regardless of what they look like. The idea of being in a clique or some form of popular group was nonexistent to me. For a while, I began to look for a home church I could attend. I came across a predominately Nigerian church, which I loved at first. As I started attending and making friends there, I realize that I didn't quite fit in. I felt people were slightly judgmental. I felt I was being judged because my name wasn't long enough, I didn't speak the language fluently enough, or I wasn't as traditional in my way of thinking, as most people who attended the church were. I experienced a level of rejection in my own community. I felt like they didn't accept me for who I was, that I just wasn't enough for them. So when I found myself in another situation along with the guy who picked someone else over me, it made me feel sad.

I remember attending my first day as a seventh grader. I was filled with so much excitement and anxiety to learn and make new friends. I remember my mom used to always tell my siblings and me that no matter what anyone does or say to us, we needed to remember that the one thing they cannot take away from us was our minds. She told us that if we worked hard enough and use our minds, we would make it far in life.

As an adult writing this book, it makes sense now, but back then, I was trying to ignore what my parents were trying to educate me. I was teased a lot because of my big nose, big lips, and big eyes. I was labeled things like "African booty scratcher." They would make fun of how dark my complexion was, that I was too dark to be seen at night. They teased me on how I spoke and told me I was only pretty enough to be dark-skinned or pretty enough for an African, but never just pretty. I never understood why there were so much hate amongst our own race and why there was always the "light-skinned" versus "dark-skinned" debate. We now live in the era where the beauty of darker skin is appreciated and celebrated. Was my skin not beautiful back then? Do I now need to accept what society considered as the idea of beauty based on different seasons? Do you see a problem here? Now I am not saying the times we are in are better than where I came from, but there is clearly an issue that needs to be addressed. We live in society that put people in a box based on how they look and the color of their skin.

Rejection comes from a place that goes beyond the exterior, beyond what you see and how you act. Rejection comes from a deeper place inside of us. It is up to you to find out the root of why you feel rejected. One of the places where rejection could stem from is your family in a form negative words that have been spoken over the course of your life. When a child grows up hearing that they would never amount to anything or achieve anything in life from their parents, that child might grow up feeling that they will not be able to accomplish anything in life. Words are so powerful! The Bible says that the power of life and death are in the tongue. Essentially, your words can produce life or death. As a parent, you have to watch what to say to your child and what you are teaching them. The Bible says that if you train up your child in the way of the Lord, they will not depart from it. We are to use or words to edify and build people, not tear down and destroy.

IN ORDER TO OVERCOME REJECTION, THERE MUST BE AN UNDERSTANDING THAT EVERY SMILING FACE ISN'T YOUR FRIEND

I didn't realize this truth until later on in life. What I went through at a young age from teasing and bullying had a negative impact on me because I subconsciously began to believe their lies and criticism. It took me a while just to reverse the cycle of the lies I've been told. Over the years, I have learned that in order to overcome rejection, there must be an understanding that every smiling face isn't your friend. Everybody in your crowd isn't always for you. The reality is, the world is filled with people who will use and think nothing of you. But it's okay! They are going to be people who will reject you, but you have got to learn to get over it. Once you feel rejected, it instantly becomes a closed door to you. If you let it, that closed door will keep you from trying again, and if you are not careful, it will hold you hostage to for the rest of your life.

There are several strategic things that I feel can help you with this, but just remember that there is no guarantee that everyone is going to accept you because we live in the real world. Whether you accept it or not, people are always going to have something to say about you whether you are doing right or wrong. First and foremost, you have to be very cautious of your connections. Be very careful about who you form relationships with. Everybody isn't worthy of being in a relationship with you. In some situations, people and jobs are not worthy of who you are. You have to realize that you belong to God! God has already created you in His image. That may be hard for you to process, but it's true (Genesis 1:27). You have to realize that He created you uniquely for His purpose, and that nothing can ever change that. It also means that there are things that He deposited inside you that you have to appreciate. When people can't appreciate the gifts and talents you bring to the table, then they are not worthy of being with you. The real issue is not that you are lacking the understanding of rejection, but rather you are lacking the knowledge of how valuable you truly are. You need to have an appreciation of your gift, your anointing, and the value of what God placed in your life. Your purpose is far too great for you to just allow it to be connected with just anybody. It's not arrogance, just awareness. Stand tall and *know* who you are and what God has given you. When you are aware of the gift, it prevents you from befriending or just hooking up with any-

> YOUR PURPOSE IS FAR TOO GREAT FOR YOU TO JUST ALLOW IT TO BE CONNECTED WITH JUST ANYBODY

body. At certain points in your life, you have to tell yourself that you are too gifted to be dealing with the kind of people who will not appreciate you and your gift. You have to make it up in your mind and say enough is enough. Create no room for self-pity or for living in your past. You have got to rise up and start seeing yourself the way God sees you.

The second thing you must do is to learn to brush off your bitterness. The problem with rejection is that it instantly makes you feel offended. You could ask yourself, "How could they not want me?" or "How could you not want this?" So now you are offended that something or someone didn't want you, especially if they choose someone else. "How did he pick her and not me?" or "How did she get the job and not me?" or "How did he get that opportunity and not me?" If you are not careful, it will leave behind bitterness that will eventually become anger. Most times, you will be able to tell those who have not gotten over some form of rejection because they are still talking about it years later. Listen, if something or someone can't accept you, then it's time for them to go. Don't let them just walk out, open the door wide open for them to leave, and then brush the residue off you so the bitterness does not begin to grow inside you. You have to do it for your own good because there will be no progress in your life if you allow it to stay with you. Don't just do it for your own good. Let it be a testimony against them. Never let them see you sweat! When you resist unforgiveness or hurt, you are essentially refusing to be bitter. What you are doing is literally testifying against the one who closed the door on you. While they thought that saying no will make you give up and throw in the towel, you are getting over it and living your best life. It will not be easy, but as you continue to do so, what you are showing is that the one who has rejected you no longer have that power over you! When you get hit, get up. Never allow anyone to hit you hard enough to keep you down. You have got to stand up and fight. Never let anyone think that they have gotten the best of you. Jump up and keep running the course.

Thirdly, you must learn to take the loss. Now this is another hard pill to swallow because rejection is offensive to your pride. Nobody wants to take a loss and be okay with it. I don't care what you say, no one is ever okay with taking a loss, but you must learn how to humble yourself for your own benefit. Sometimes it's tough to feel like you are chosen by God. With all the gifts and talents you have, you still feel rejected. You feel that way because pride won't let you understand how that can happen. You may have all the right things, look the right way, got a lot going on for yourself, and say, "How could they still not want me"? You have to be careful because pride tells you that you are too gifted not to get what you want, and because you want it, it should want you. Pride says, "With my résumé, I'm supposed to get in." Pride says, "With everything I got going on, I just know they are going to accept me." Pride will keep you in a place where you feel rejected. Pride won't let you walk away from your rejection. If you don't, you will become hostage to it and start questioning yourself as to why things didn't work outs. Once again, you have to learn how to take a loss because it's a part of life. No matter how gifted you are, understand that every job you desire will not be yours, every relationship or marriage will not always work, not every friendship will last forever, and everything you desire will not always be good for you. When you are in a place of rejection, you have to know when it's time to leave. You don't have to argue, you don't have to go back and forth. Don't beg or plead, just pack your stuff up physically, emotionally, financially, and spiritually. It's time for you to leave. In order to get over it, you have to get away from it. If you stay, you will never get healed from it. The only way to get over rejection is get out of a place where you felt rejected and connect yourself to something else.

IN ORDER TO GET OVER IT, YOU HAVE TO GET AWAY FROM IT. IF YOU STAY, YOU WILL NEVER GET HEALED FROM IT

Lastly, you have to perceive another possibility. If someone doesn't receive your gifts and who you are as a person, then you need to understand that they are just not for you. You need to find others who will be accepting of your gifts. Don't get trapped in one place because God has something better for you elsewhere. The problem is, when people feel rejected, they typically ask God the wrong questions. Instead of asking God why it happened, ask Him what's next for you. It's not why you didn't get it, but what else is in store for you because God always has another possibility. It doesn't matter what door has been closed. God has another job, another program, another friend, another relationship, or another marriage for you. Do not act all rejected, sad, and depressed simply because one door was closed in your life. God is the ruler and the Creator of the heaven and the earth. He could make something out of nothing. If God created the earth in just seven days, then believe that He will certainly create another opportunity for you. God is a problem solver. He is in control of your life. No amount of rejection can keep Him away from loving you. Just remember, the reason some people have turned against you and walked away from you without any reason has nothing to do with you. God removed them from your life because they cannot go where He is taking you. You have got to let them go and keep moving because something greater is coming. So if you are struggling through rejection, pray the prayer below constantly, and I know God will see you though.

THE REASON SOME PEOPLE HAVE TURNED AWAY FROM YOU WITHOUT ANY REASON HAS NOTHING TO DO WITH YOU

Prayer

The Lord is close to the brokenhearted, he saves those whose spirit are broken hearted, he saves those who spirit has been crushed. People who do what is right may have many problems, but the Lord will solve them all. He will protect their very bones, not of them will broken. (Psalm 34:17–20)

Dear heavenly Father, I come to You today, asking that you heal me completely and that you make me whole again. You say in Your word that You are close to the brokenhearted, and You save those who spirits have been crushed. I admit that You haven't always been the first person I turn to for help, but I am coming to You now. I am asking that You help me. Please, Lord, help me to make better decisions, as I am trusting You to fix and right all my wrongs. Protect me as You have said, Lord. In Jesus' name, amen.

If the world hates you, remember that it hated me first. If you belonged to the world, then it would love you as it loves its own. But i have chosen you out of the world, so you don't belong to it. That is why the world hates you. (John 15:18–19)

The Lord Jesus is the stone that loves. The people of the world did not want this stone, but He was worth much. So come to Him, as you also are living stones. (1 Peter 2:4–5)

Dear Father, I now understand the purpose of the rejection that I have received. I now understand that I have to go through rejection because the world rejected You first. I know now that I am your child, and because they rejected You, they are going to reject me. But, Lord, as You persevere through it, I ask that You give me the same strength and the same grace. You have called me chosen with a purpose in Your word, Lord. Feeling rejected or unwanted help me remember that no matter what the world thinks, I am chosen by You.

If my father and my mother reject me, the Lord will take me in. (Psalm 27:10)

Dear God, it's hard for me to honestly accept that You accept me. This is mostly because of how I was raised. If you know how my parents are, you know everything. I didn't receive the kind of love I needed from my mother and my father, so I admit that hearing You say You will take me in is very strange to me. You are the God who keeps His promises and is true to His word. So, Father, even though I feel rejected by my parents, you'll take me in. I am asking you to take me in, Lord, and wrap me under Your wing. Teach me the definition of love, teach me how to love, and fill me up with Your love, Lord, so I can be able to pour that love into others. I want to thank You because even in the rejection, I know now that You will always be there for me and You will never forsake me. Help me, Lord, to see myself the way You see me. In Jesus' name, amen.

So what should we say about this? If God is for us, then no one can defeat us. (Romans 8:31)

You are blessed when people hate you and are cruel to you. You are blessed when they say that you are evil because you belong to the Son of Man. At that time, be full of joy because you have a great reward in heaven. Their fathers were cruel to the prophets in the same way these people are cruel to you. (Luke 6:22–23)

Lord, I want thank You because I know now that if You are for me, then no one can be against me and no one can defeat me in anything. Lord, I am human. I must admit to my weakness. You say in Your word that I am blessed when people are talking about me. You want me to rejoice in that because there is great reward for me in heaven. Lord, honestly, I ask that You continue to strengthen me in my times of rejection. Help me and teach me to count it as joy and to have reassurance that You will see me through because I belong to you. In Jesus' name, amen!

Can a woman forget the baby she nurses? Can she feel no kindness for the child she gave birth to? Even if she could forget her children, I will not forget you. See, I have written your name in my hand (Isaiah 49:15–16)

I say this because I know…I have good plans for you. I don't plan to hurt you. I plan to give you hope and a good future. Then you will call my name. You will come to me and pray to

me. And I will listen to you. You will search for
me. And when you search for me with all your
heart, you will find me! I will let you find me,
says the lord! (Jeremiah 29:11–14)

*Dear God, I want to thank You so much for this love that You speak
of. It is evident in Your scripture that You will not leave me or forget me,
so I will hold You to that, Lord. It's amazing to read and now know that
You have written my name in Your hand. That alone means that I must
be special to You. I thank You. I have been dealing with rejection for a
while now, and I don't really know how to seek any help from anyone.
God, You are very much aware of all the trials that I have to face in my
life, but I know You are working things out for my good. I thank You,
Father, that regardless of how damaged I am or how messed up I think
my past is, it's good to know that You still have good plans for me. I thank
You, Lord, for Your intentions of not planning to hurt me but to give me
hope and a good future. Teach me, Lord, how to seek and find You with
my whole heart and to build a consistent relationship with You. I have no
idea where and how to start, but I am trusting You to guide me through
this process in Jesus' name.*

You are here to defend the defenseless, to
make sure that underdogs get a fair break; your
job is to stand up for the powerless, and prose-
cute all those who exploit them. (Psalm 82:3–4
MSG)

*Dear God, I am coming to You today because there have been times
in my life where I have felt defenseless in certain things and situations
that were out of my control. I have been holding on to some of those
things for a while because of the pain and how I was affected by it. Your
word says that You will defend the defenseless, that You provide and stand
up for the powerless. Defend me, O God, and vindicate me for all the
unfairness I have had thus far. I am asking You to fight for me, Lord. I
need You to fight for me because I cannot do it by myself, and I certainly*

cannot win it alone. I give it to you, Lord, and I thank You for defending me, amen.

There are so many ways that rejection feeds and plays into our lives. It's important that we know how to address those issues. Praying these prayers isn't going to magically make your problems go away. It's not just praying that will make it work, it's believing and trusting the one you are praying to. Prayer is a dialogue between you and God, and it could be done through so many forms. You can pray out loud, pray quietly, pray silently, or worship. God will always be there to hear you out no matter what your struggles are. Having faith in what you pray for will always equate to miracles. If you pray about something, believe in it, and expect that it is going to happen, then it will. Believe that you are free from all forms of rejection and God loves you more than you know, and you will indeed be free.

Loss

Heartbreak and rejection were easy to write because I experienced those two things. However, when it came to the topic of loss, I hadn't experienced it at the time. I didn't want to deliver something or share something with you that I was yet to experience so I removed it, but God obviously had other plans. The irony!

On February 11 2019, my oldest brother Milade was found dead in his apartment. Although I know without a doubt that he is resting in heaven, it still didn't make it any less painful that I will not be seeing my brother for a very long time. He died at age thirty, leaving behind my two-year-old niece and his wife of four years. I was twenty-nine. My younger siblings were twenty-three and eighteen. Out of all the siblings, my brother and I were the closest in the bunch. We grew up together in Nigeria, only two years apart, and were inseparable. He was not only my brother, but he was also my best friend. I started to write this topic twenty-eight days after he passed away. Up until then, I had never experienced loss before. I was always the one who heard about loss and felt empathy for the families involved. I often said on so many occasions, "Sorry for your loss" but never truly knew and understood the impact of those words. It wasn't until I lost my brother that I began to understand what those words meant.

Death is never anything that I would wish upon anyone. Losing your loved one is like a big wound that you can't cover up. It's an emotional pain that can cause you to feel sick physically, emotionally, and mentally. It will take a while for it to heal. As of this writing, I'm still grieving. The process of grieving varies from person to person, but I know for me thus far, the process has not been easy at all. When I first found out that my brother passed away, I was at work. I was numb, speechless, and in shock. It took me a while to learn how to deal and cope with it. I was the type of person who didn't do much sulking. If the job wasn't working out, I move on. If the relationship wasn't working out, I move on and get over it. I remember feeling like I was losing control of everything, and I hated it. I was experiencing so many emotions all at once. It was extremely terrifying. Dealing with the loss of my brother and learning how to find healthy coping mechanisms was something new for me.

Heartbreak and rejection are, in itself, an excruciating thing to go through, but losing someone is a different kind of pain. It completely shakes up your entire world to pieces that only God can put back together. I honestly don't know how people go through this by themselves. I had sometimes heard people say that they know someone who died of a broken heart after a loved one passed away. I've even heard stories of individuals committing suicide after their love one died because they cannot endure that pain. It wasn't until I lost my brother that I understood the phrase "dying from a broken heart." When you have a broken heart, you feel like this because the thought of not having your loved one around causes you more pain.

The idea of suicide doesn't sound that bad, but killing yourself (or anybody) means there is no bringing that person back. Suicide is an act of selfishness because you didn't breathe life into your body, God did that! God gave you life as a gift, so it's not up to you to end your life without the permission of the Giver. Everyone has an appointment with death. Unless it's your time to go, taking your own life is telling God you don't trust Him enough to see you out of the situation you are in. Not only that, taking your own life could result to trauma for the loved ones you leave behind. Is it fair for them to experience the same pain and heartbreak you're experiencing? NO! None of it is fair. Taking your life is not up to you, that is completely up to God. He doesn't need you to help Him take your life. The fact that you are still living is proof that there is a purpose for you. Whatever that purpose is, whatever that assignment is has not yet been completed, so it is not up to you to take your own life.

I had to accept that my brother's purpose on this earth was complete. That is why God took him, but even realizing that was not easy at all. I had to realize eventually that life itself is very fleeting. The people and things around us that we care for and love is a gift of God, but it's only temporary. The Bible states that everything good comes from God. So that good job, that good husband, that good wife, that good brother or sister, or that good thing comes from God. He can take it away from us at any given time. But the concept of God being the giver and the taker is a hard truth to swallow because of the emotional attachment we have with that person or thing. As discussed earlier, I said heartbreak is a pain that you experience emotionally. It cannot be quantifiable, but it can be contained. Eventually, you get over a heartbreak and move on with your life. However, a broken heart from the loss of a loved one is different. It's a pain that takes time to heal and a memory you will never forget as long as you live. But there's hope. After eight months, I am thankful to say that the impact and the pain has subsided a lot, but his memory is forever engraved in my mind and heart. The death of my brother left me physically weak. I had no desire to do anything, and I was tired all the time. All I wanted to do was eat and sleep. During this time, I gained so much of I called "grief weight." I ate pretty much anything in sight. It was terrible for my body, but it made me feel slightly better emotionally. I was crying all the time.

People would say to me, "Do not skip the grieving process" or "You have to be strong for your family." I honestly didn't know what that was. I am the second oldest out of four. When my brother died, I felt like I had a bigger responsibility to my siblings and my family. I felt like I had to do more and be there for them like never before. It was already troubling enough that this was my reality, but I also felt pressured when people would tell me that I needed to "be strong." I hated that. It made me feel like I was pressured not to be vulnerable, that I had to be there for my family. But for me, that was inevitable. That is and will always be my job. I had no choice. I didn't want to hear how strong I was. What I needed was for people to show support and tell me that it is okay to cry, that it's okay to be vulnerable, and that it's okay not to be okay. I had some friends tell me that they didn't know how to respond to me because I am always so together or so strong all the time. Although I know they meant well, it upset me. I am human first before I am a woman. That alone makes me susceptible to emotions. I don't know why people feel like we aren't supposed to show any sign of weakness. What people don't realize is that in time like these, the strongest people are the weakest. Even though they are there for everyone else, they also need someone to be there for them. Now I am not saying that I didn't have any support from my friends and I would be remiss of me if I didn't share with you of all the outpouring love and support that my family received at that time. It was truly overwhelming. From friends and coworkers to random strangers, the love was real.

Weeks into Milade's death, I couldn't really do anything or feel anything at the time. Eight months in, there were still certain songs that remind me of that day that triggers the memory of him. I stayed with my parents for several weeks after he died, just being around family and friends. However, as much of a blessing spending time with them was, I had to come to the realization that this was my new normal. When I finally moved back to my place, I felt an incredible sense of loneliness that I had never experienced before. At that point in my life, I wasn't dating. I made a decision that I would be patient and focus on my relationship with God. But the loneliness made me feel very empty inside. I realized that I didn't want be alone. I wanted to be held. I wanted companionship, not just from anyone, but from a man. But not just any man, I wanted it to be someone I could trust, someone who will not use my vulnerability to their advantage. Believe it or not, men like this actually exist.

Don't get me wrong, I had my closest girlfriends rally around me. There was an incredible amount of support from a lot of people, but for some reason, I needed something more. Frankly, all I wanted was to be cuddled and to be around someone that I can be transparent with. As I sat on my couch, I no longer felt strong. I no longer felt like I was the superwoman people were making me out to be. For once, I wanted to give my cape to a man who can help me with this burden, and I yearned for that affection like ever before. I truly believed that God made me go through this process alone because He wanted me to lean on Him as my source and strength, not any man. God wanted me to see that He was all that I needed, that He could do far more than what any man can ever do for me.

Now I have always had male friends. As a matter of fact, there is a higher percentage of male than female in my circle so getting a man was never a problem, but I didn't just want anybody to be with me. I was emotional and vulnerable, but I was still smart. I didn't just want anyone to take advantage of me, but they certainly tried it. The level of men that came out of nowhere when I was grieving was unbelievable. I'm not talking about my guy friends. I'm talking about guys who knew me in passing or reached out through social media to wine and dine me. They told me they wanted to "be there" for me. Not to say all those men had ill intentions, but I thought it was interesting to see how some men can prey on a woman's vulnerability. Ladies, if you are reading this, be warned of men or people who come out of nowhere to take advantage of your vulnerability. Loss will make you open and susceptible to a lot of things, so remember to be cautious of who you are surrounding yourself with. This also goes for men as well. God, being the good Father and friend that He is, knew what I was feeling and sent me a word.

> *I call you back. I call you back into my arms. Don't doubt what I've made and how I've made you. Stay close to me. Hear my voice where light falls in shadows, where noise rises, and you aren't sure how you could ever truly hear me. You hear me. I am near.*
>
> *My daughter, being with me, hearing my voice, and letting me lead you requires turning over*

your heart. Rise up now and see where I am. I am right here.

No excuses now. You are designed for a relationship with me. You are designed to crave connection with a community of people who know you and love you. You are designed to be known and understood. You are designed to be loved. Loved. I love you perfectly and completely. There is no other love you need to chase down. I will bring people into your life who are designed to love too. They will be called to love you and reflect me to you. They are called to help you hear Me. They are called to help you walk straight where I walk straight and turn when I turn.

You, my daughter, are not made to be alone. So if you are lonely, misunderstood, and long for an arm around you, a friend to sit beside you, and a person to lift you up when you are weary and down, call on me, my dear one. Call on your Father who made you and designed you to yearn for connection. Take a risk, go on the adventure I call you to, and trust the safe places I've created for you so others can see me, hear me, and lean on me too.

It's not better to be independent and solitary all the time. Come to me and find me in my home, my church. I will show you how to move forward. I will show you how to trust. I will protect your heart as you stay close to me, take risks, and head into what feels dangerous and unknown. This world is dangerous, but you have a helper in me.

The ironic thing about this is that if you believe in God, you know He is omnipresent, meaning He is everywhere. Not only that, but He is always listening and hearing our thoughts, and constantly respective to what we think. The message I got was from a group I follow called Loop, created by Jennifer J. Camp. She sends prophetic messages to the group weekly. During my grieving process, God used her to speak comfort into my life. When I would think that all that I wanted was an arm around me, God saw fit to send me a message to assure me that He was with me in this process. For the next few days, I decided that instead of seeking for a man to hold me in the most difficult time in my life, God was showing me that He was all I ever needed. People love and do things with conditions, but the love of God is unconditional.

My mother had always been God's voice in my life. When my brother died, I began to think of my own life and how short it really is. As I stated earlier, everyone has an appointment with death. As a matter of fact, there is a time for everything:

> *There is a time for everything, and a season for every activity under the heavens: a time to be born and a time to die, a time to plant and a time to uproot, a time to kill and a time to heal, a time to tear down and a time to build, a time to weep and a time to laugh, a time to mourn and a time to dance, a time to scatter stones and a time to gather them, a time to embrace and a time to refrain from embracing, a time to search and a time to give up, a time to keep and a time to throw away, a time to tear and a time to mend, a time to be silent and a time to speak, a time to love and a time to hate, a time for war and a time for peace.* (Ecclesiastes 3:1–8 NIV)

God said that there is a right time for everything, time to be born, time to die, time to heal, time to build, etc. It got me into thinking about my brother's life. I realized that maybe it was his time to go. Maybe he had already served his purpose, and God saw it fit to call him home. Then I started to think about my life and if I am living in my purpose. As I stated earlier, my mother had always been God's voice to me, but my brother's passing made me realize that I needed to learn what God sounds like for myself. I realized that my mom isn't always going to be around, so I needed to practice listening and hearing Him myself. With so many emotions, I began to pray more here and there. Let me just say that when it comes to prayer, there is no perfect or accurate way we need to pray. God is not concerned about the posture of your body or the ramblings of big or sweet words. He is concerned about the posture of your heart.

Prayer is the art of communication. Literally, it is just talking to God as you would a person or a friend, conveying your thoughts, feelings, or emotions when you have no words. Sometimes when you want to pray, you may not know what to say, but it's okay because God has given us His Holy Spirit who communicates to God for us when we fall short of words. He will pray on your behalf. Romans 8:26 (ISV) states, "But the Spirit also helps us in our weaknesses, since we do not know how to pray as we should. But the Spirit himself intercedes for us with groans too deep for words." God can see what's in the heart of people. He knows what is in our mind because the Spirit speaks to God for His people. Isn't this amazing to know that the Holy Spirit is speaking to God on your behalf! I still wasn't able to read and pray to God like I should have, but it didn't stop God from speaking to me. Here is the second message He had for me from my Loop group:

> My daughter, listening to me is a practice I want to teach you. First, take a deep breath and again. Slow down now. Wait a bit for me. Trust that I am here. As you listen to the sound of your breath, as you feel your lungs expand—pushing the air throughout your body, your chest rising and falling—think about inhaling me and breathing me in. I am as close as your breath. I have created you so I am in you and part of you. I am the natural rhythm of your breathing.
>
> Inhale. Breathe deeply now. Be aware of the sound of your body inhaling. One breath and then another. Think of me when you breathe. Breathing is something you take for granted, isn't it? You assume the air will be there for you to breathe in,

that your lungs will have what they need so that you can live another day. Your body needs air, but you also need me. Your soul needs me more than your body needs air. I am what you are desperate for. You are not alive without me. Your soul does not breathe without me. I am fresh air in tired lungs that live to expand and take in this fresh air I offer.

Oh, daughter, breathe me in. All the way now. This is the sound of my voice in you as you breath Me in and out. It's so simple, your thinking of me is the beginning of listening to me, knowing I am in you, and I love you.

There is no magic formula for listening well to me. There is no complicated list of suggestions to follow. I have no checklist, no program to offer you. But I have myself to give to you again and again. When I give you myself, I give you all of me. I don't hold myself back from you. I do not set myself apart. I want no separation from you. I give you all of Me for I want all of you So breathe, my child. Breathe me in. All of me. Think about how much you need me, and my love for you will pour out. You will know me more, and my goodness will flood your heart. Then you will know even more whose you are and who you love. How good it is to breathe air that is pure, air that is fresh, and air that sustains.

Then the Lord God formed the man of dust from the ground and breathed into his nostrils the breath of life, and the man became a living creature. (Genesis 2:7)

With plenty of prayers, crying, and lonely nights, I'm happy to say that nine months after my brother's death, my heart doesn't hurt as much. Granted, I understand that people deal with death differently. Some are completely numb to it, get busy, and get on with their lives. Others are so distraught for years to come that they cannot seem to pick themselves up. So you see, everybody experiences this trauma differently. I was told that I had to go through the stages of grief, that I should go see a grief counselor. I was told a lot of things that just didn't work for me. I am not saying that the grieving process won't work for you or that getting counsel won't help because I do think that you need time to heal and find the most constructive way to deal with your new normal. My advice would be to move to beat of your own drum. Figure out your best healthy coping mechanisms that works well for you, not what someone is telling you to do.

Personally, praying and reading my Bible helped a lot. It was not easy at first because my body didn't feel like doing it, but I took it one step at a time. My advice for you would be to do the same thing. God *is* the only one who can literally remove that pain away. That doesn't mean that you will completely forget about your loved one who died, but with each step you take toward God, He will make greater steps to come toward you. I read the Bible app on my phone, which can be found in the app store. This app is very resourceful. I was able to find devotional on how to deal with loss and grief. A few times a week, I would make an effort to read something to help my mind. Days turned into weeks and weeks turned into months. Today, eighteen months in, I can think about my brother and smile because I know he is no longer in pain. I can think about the memories and cry because I can't make new ones with him, but the pain is far less than it started. Yes, the memory doesn't go away. Yes, you are going to go through a series of emotion where you have highs and lows, but remember that it's okay not to be okay. Also remember that the only one who can fix a broken heart is God. The prayer below is to help you and show you how to start.

Prayer

Blessed be the God and Father of our Lord Jesus Christ, the father of sympathy (pity and mercy) and the God [Who is the source] of every comfort (consolation and encouragement) Who comforts (consoles and encourages) us in every trouble (calamity and affliction), so that we may also be able to comfort (console and encourage) those who are in any kind of trouble or distress, with the comfort with which we ourselves are comforted by God. (2 Corinthians 1:3–4)

Heavenly Father, I am hurting. Your words says You are the Father of sympathy and the source of all comfort. I'm hurting pretty bad, Lord, and I need you to comfort me. I need to feel You right now because this pain is unbearable. I miss my loved one so much, I honestly do not know what to do with my life. It is too much, Lord! I am asking that You console me during this time and be my source of strength during this time. In Jesus' name, amen!

The Lord is close to those who are of a broken heart, and saves such that are crushed with sorrow. (Psalm 34:18)

Dear God, my heart is broken and crushed because I lost my loved one. Your word says that You are indeed close to those who have a broken heart. I need to feel You, Lord, because I am losing it. I do not know how much of this pain I can take. Please help me, Lord, and draw close to me. I am not sure how long I will feel this pain, but I am asking You to help me through the process and guide me on what you would have me do.

You're blessed when you feel you've lost what is most dear to you. Only then can you embrace the One most dear to you. (Matthew 5:4 MSG)

My grace is enough; it's all you need. My strength comes into its own in your weakness. (2 Corinthians 12:9)

Jesus, Your word says that I am blessed when I have lost what's dear to me because only then will I be able to embrace the One dear to me.

I'm confused, Lord. I'm angry and hurt. You mean to tell me that even though I lost my loved one, I am still blessed? And it had to happen so I can embrace You? I need you, Lord. I don't get all of this. I certainly do not feel blessed, but you are the Almighty God, and You know more than me. Your ways are not my ways, and Your thoughts are not my thoughts. Lord, whatever my blessings will be throughout this grieving process, please show me. I do not want to feel this pain anymore. I am sad, Lord, I am hurting so much. Please bless me as I continue to draw closer to you. Be my strength, Lord, when I am weak. You said your grace is all I need. Well, I need You to show me how. In Jesus' name, amen!

Praise be to God and the Father of our Lord Jesus Christ. God is the Father who is full of mercy. And he is the God of comfort, he comforts us every time we are in trouble, so that we can comfort others who have trouble. We can comfort them with the same comfort that God gives us. (2 Corinthians 1:3–5)

Dear God, Your words clearly describe the experiences and the pain that I am feeling now is really for someone else. Lord, I know that You are able to turn my situation around, but please help me through this process, so I can be in a position to help another person who also lost their loved one. Help me with my pain and emotions. Sometimes it's hard for me to feel or think anything. Sometimes I do not even want to eat or get out the bed, and You are asking me to go through this to be so I can comfort someone else, lord? I don't know how I'll do it. I do not have the answers. But, Lord, the only way that I can comfort another human being experiencing this pain is if You comfort me, Lord. Please take over my mind, my thoughts, and my emotions and give me the grace and strength to make it through, so I can be there for someone else. In Jesus' name, amen.

He heals the brokenhearted and bandages their wounds. (Psalm 147:3–4)

Lord, this kind of heartbreak is very unbearable for me to cope and deal with. Your word clearly states that You heal those whose hearts are broken and bandage their wounds. Lord, to be quiet honest, I don't know how you are going to do it, but I am asking You to please heal and mend my broken heart during this time. Losing the one I love is an emotional pain that only you can heal, Lord. It's invisible to the naked eye, but I know You see the depth of this pain. I'm giving it to You, lord, and I am still asking You to heal my broken heart according to You word in Psalm 147.

For there is a right time for everything. Everything on earth has it special season. There is a time to be born and a time to die. There is a time to plant and a time to pull up plants. There is a time to kill and a time to heal. There is a time to destroy and a time to build. There is a time to cry and a time to laugh. There is a time to be sad and a time to dance. There is a time to throw away stones and a time to gather them. There is a time to hug and time not to hug. There is a time to look for something and a time to stop looking for it. There is s time to keep things and a time to throw things away. There is a time to be silent and a time to speak. There is a time to love and a time to hate. There is a time of war and a time of peace. (Ecclesiastes 3:1–8)

Dear Lord, apparently there is a time for everything to take place in life. You mentioned a time to be born and a time to die. Lord, as hard as it is to say, I know that You are both the giver and the taker, even in this moment when I think about my love one who passed away. I suppose it was the right time for that to happen, but that still does not soften the blow and the pain that I feel right now. But, Lord, since You said that there is a right time for everything, I ask that You bring me into the time of laugher again. I am sad currently, but I ask that You see me through this time until I get to the time of dancing that You speak of. Even though right now with the pain that I am feeling, a time of joy and complete healing may seem a little impossible. You are the one who will make the all things possible. I ask that You give me the grace to trust You in this process in Jesus' name.

But the Lord said to me, "My grace is enough for you. When you are weak, then my power is made perfect in you." (2 Corinthians 2:9 ICB)

Dear God, Your word is saying that Your grace is enough. Honestly, Lord, I want to believe that it is, but at present, it's hard to believe that this pain will pass. It's hard to believe that I can come out this battle. But here I am, and I know you are not one to lie, so please give me the grace I need in the season. Only You know why my loved one had to die, Lord. Bring me to a place of acceptance and give me Your grace to keep me going on a daily basis. Please be my strength when I am weak because there are going to be days, Lord, that I may not make it. I need You to come through for me as You always do. In Jesus' name, amen.

2

Living Under Sexual Thoughts (LUST)

Listen, this Christian walk is not a walk in the park at all. I don't want you all to think that everything goes smoothly when you decided to follow Christ. If anything, things may get worse. The difference is, you are now connected to the life source who can and will deliver you from whatever you are struggling with. You have to know that God's love for you is unconditional. That means there is nothing you can do, good or bad, to make Him stop loving you.

I have already told you all a little bit about my dating history in my previous chapter, but I think I want to be a little bit more detailed as to why we, as human beings, lust after another person, even as God-fearing Christians. Before I go into that, let's see how God feels about lust. You see, the purpose of this book is to set people free from themselves so they can be the best version of themselves. In order for you to really understand what this is, you have to first take a look on how God feels about it. The Bible says in Matthew 5:28–30 (ICB), "But I tell you that if anyone looks at a woman with lust, he has already committed adultery in his mind. If your right eye causes you to sin, then take it out and throw it away. It is better to lose one part of your body than to have your whole body thrown into hell."

> BUT I TELL YOU THAT IF ANYONE LOOKS AT A WOMAN WITH LUST, HE HAS ALREADY COMMITTED ADULTERY IN HIS MIND

You can clearly see how serious God takes this. Logically, when we lust after someone, the first thing we see is what the person looks like. Then as you water the seed, lust creeps in when you start imagining or fantasizing about what you want to happen sexually with this person. Now keep in mind that a sin is a sin. In the eyes of God, there is no greater or lesser sin. He sees sin all the same, wrong and dirty! God hates this particular sin so much that He literally tells you to cut off a body part. That's extreme, right? Can you imagine taking both your eyes out every time you look at someone lustfully or maybe cutting off your fingers because its causes you to sin? Can you imagine using your thumb to navigate a pornographic site and then cutting it off? This may seem very harsh and a bit extreme when you think about it, but that is how serious God takes it. Ultimately, God is saying that He would rather you make it to heaven with several body parts missing than for you to burn in hell for eternity. Now this also doesn't mean that anytime you lust for someone, you will need to cut off a body part. I believe that analogy was spoken figuratively.

I want to be clear that if you want to be free from this area of sin, the first thing that you have to understand is that you aren't the one with the problem. It's your heart. However, you shouldn't take His grace for granted on the account that He's only judging your heart. For me personally, this was the area in my life where I struggled the most, masturbation and, in some ways, porn. At this point in my life, I was celibate. I wanted to do the right thing and live a godly life, but it was extremely difficult and challenging. I knew having sex and fulfilling any sexual desires was not pleasing to God outside of the context of marriage, but that didn't stop my body for thinking, feeling, and wanting it. Now according to society, sex plays a big part in a relationship. However, if you are a true believer and a follower of Jesus Christ, you { **THE REAL CAUSE IS YOUR HEART** would know that sex with someone who isn't your husband or a wife is a sin in the eyes of God. Christian or not, we are all guilty of it, for the most part. Like I said, I struggled with masturbation fueled with porn. This started at a very young age, maybe when I was around eleven. I remember turning on the TV one night and seeing disturbing images of people doing things I had not been exposed to. I remember not knowing what I was looking at. I didn't really pay any attention to it. I also didn't tell my dad what I had seen. I just went on my merry way. What I didn't know was that I had opened the door for a seed to be planted in my mind that would fester over time and become a fruit in my life.

When I got to college, I had just gotten out of a long-term relationship. I was adjusting to life as a college kid. One day, it happened! I was in my dorm room when I become very horny. It was as if something attacked me or came over me, but it was pretty intense. I started making videos of pleasuring myself for fun. I became excited and wanted more! So I grabbed my computer and began browsing the web. I discovered all sorts of porn. A mere twenty minutes turned into several hours to the point where I missed my class that evening. I remember being heavily engrossed in it that nothing else mattered but that moment. The things I saw that day sowed a lustful seed in my life that manifested throughout the course of my adulthood even after college.

Watching porn or masturbating may seem normal in a relationship, but it really isn't. There are some interesting things that happen in your mind when you masturbate or when you watch pornography. It is like a drug that is addictive. As with most addictions, it comes with no warning signs. Once you start, it will be very difficult to stop. Trust me, I tried to stop on my own with many failed attempts until I discovered a way out. The problem is not why you can't stop having those nasty thoughts or can't stop masturbating, but the problem is your heart. First, you have to dig deeper and really think about when it started. Like me, some of you might have stumbled on something that popped up on your TV. For some, it could be rape or exposure through magazine. I want to you think of your five senses: what you see, what you hear, what you feel, what you taste, and what you touch. I want you think of your senses as mentioned and begin to think of which part triggers your lustful act. Think about it, write it down, and then pray on it. Ultimately, your thoughts and actions are not the root of the problem. The real cause is your heart. Once you allow God to deal with content of your heart, you will begin to see physical changes.

There is a story I read online about an old man and his grandson about the constant battle that happens in our minds. He said, "My son, the battle is between two wolves inside us all. One is evil (anger, envy, jealousy, sorrow, regret, greed, arrogance, self-pity, guilt, resentment, inferiority, lies, false pride, superiority, ego, etc.). The other is good (joy, peace, love, hope, serenity, humility, kindness, benevolence, empathy, generosity, truth, compassion, and faith)." The son thought about it for a minute and asked, "Which one wins?" The old man responded. "The one that you feed." So the real question is, which one do you feed the most? The *you* who is love, joy, and happiness and have the power to say no or the *you* who decides to give in to your sexual desire each time it creeps up.

When I started writing this section, I came up with acronym to describe the term *lust*:

- Living
- Under
- Sexual
- Thoughts

The power of lust is very real. The reason why it happens so frequently is because people are constantly living under sexual thoughts (LUST). Some of the ladies reading this book might know a guy or two who always think about sex or talks about sex. I'm pretty sure there are men who are reading this book as well who know women whose primary desire is just sex. Now don't get me wrong, sex in itself is a beautiful thing created by God. God knew it was so beautiful and so powerful that the only way He will approve and protect you from all the dangers that come with it is if it's in the context of marriage. God will not bless sex outside of that. To be quite honest, you are also opening yourself up to so many side effects that are both physical and spiritual. Physical side effects such as sexually transmitted infections and spiritual side effect such as soul-ties.

The good news is that if you are living in lust and you want to change, there is hope for you. There is an old phrase women used to say when they are dating a man they don't want to be sexually active with, "The kitchen is closed." If you were to ask a random stranger what the purpose of a kitchen is, I guarantee that the most common answer would be "to cook." Some might even say "to store things away" or "to create something out of nothing." So then what happens when a kitchen is closed or under construction? Realistically speaking, it means there is no kind of activity going on that kitchen or maybe it's not ready for public view. Now when a woman use that phrase, there could be one or two motives behind it, abstinence or celibacy. These two words, although they have very similar meaning, are very different. To abstain from something means to withhold yourself from something you otherwise want or enjoy. It could be alcohol, shopping, any guilty pleasures, and, of course, sex! When someone says they are abstaining from sex, it simple means they have chosen to wait to have sex until they found someone deserving enough for them. Now to be celibate is usually tied to religious beliefs. This happens when someone, usually a Christian, decides to forgo sex until marriage because according to God, the pre-marital sex is a sin. Being a celibate is a personal commitment and decision you make before God that you will wait until you are within the constitution of a marriage before having sex. Sounds easy, but believe me, it is an extremely difficult thing that no one can go through unless you receive grace from God.

This I know too well because I'm on the celibacy journey as I am writing this book. I took this path a very long time ago. The journey has been rewarding but also extremely difficult. The idea of wanting to be celibate started when I took my walk with God a lot more seriously. I wanted to practice what I preached and do what I thought was right. Now before I go any further, I would like to debunk all the churches in general that preach sex is a bad thing. Sex was invented by God, not by Trey Songz or your favorite R and B artist. God made it, and for that reason alone, it's good. However, He made it in the context of a marriage between a man and a woman with very good reasons. "For this reason a man will leave his father and mother and be united to his wife, and the two will become one flesh" (Matthew 19:5 NIV). God knew sex was so powerful that the only two people who should be having it is a man and his wife. In the era we live in, people use the analogy of "testing a car before driving it" in reference to having sex with someone before you get married.

I know a lot of guys who prioritize sex over everything will agree with that statement because they feel like they are scared of the idea of putting sex on the shelf in a relationship that leads to marriage and not meet the expectations they desire. Now if you are one of those guys, then you might as well stop reading the book right now. This book is for those who struggle and want to be better. I personally think when you remove sex temporarily from the table, you learn about the other person on an emotional and a spiritual level, but you have to be equipped enough to handle it. The only person who can give you the tools is God who made sex. God knew exactly what he was talking about when He said sex should only be in a context of a marriage. He knew you would struggle because of how strong that bond is. But do you not know that there is nothing you give up for God that He will not multiply? If you are a guy in a relationship whose partner is suggesting the idea of celibacy, and your main concern is the disappointment that may occur when you're married, then I personally don't think that's a real problem. For starters, if you are in a Christian relationship with a deeply emotional and strong spiritual connection, then that's already half the battle. If you can come together with those two attributes and get married, then God will bless it. I guarantee you that the sex will be wonderful. If your spouse needs a little teaching to sharpen their skills to make you happy, then you teach them! You both literally have *forever* to make each other happy. It's all about trusting God and having proper communication. What if you get married and the sex is the best you have ever had? Don't you know if you decide to step out on faith and make that commitment to God that He will bless you with someone who will satisfy you? Do you not trust God enough to give your heart's desires? I am not saying that it will be easy, but it will be worth it. If you want to be better with your spiritual life and grow your relationship with God, then you have to hate sin to be free from it. Be warned!

Now as a young Christian woman, I started to date pretty young. I was always taught not to have sex, but with not good enough reason. As I became a young teenager, the urges to have sex became stronger. As an adult, it was all I wanted to do. When I became celibate, however, I decided to not have any sex, but it didn't stop me from wanting to do other things. I was naive enough to think that just because I am choosing not to have sex, I was good. I was wrong, and it made my struggle even harder. Someone once asked me if masturbation was a sin. My response was "Can you say a prayer to God before you masturbate like you would do before you ate a meal? Can you actually utter the words 'Father in heaven, I ask You to be with me today as I masturbate'?" Think about it and answer that question honestly. Think about what kind of emotions you might be experiencing. Would you be able do that? If you aren't able to pray to God before you perform sexual act, then you know that it's something that God will not be happy with. But if that answer isn't good enough for you, then refer to 1 Corinthians 6:18, "Flee from sexual immorality. Every other sin a person commits is outside the body, but the sexually immoral person sins against his own body." Those are God's word in black and white! Masturbation, oral sex, intercourse, or any sexual acts a person does outside their body is a sin.

> CAN YOU SAY A PRAYER TO GOD BEFORE YOU MASTURBATE LIKE YOU WOULD DO BEFORE YOU ATE A MEAL?

I need you to remember that the one you feed will always win. If talking to God like that about that subject makes you feel uneasy, then you already have you answer. The Bible says that even though some of us act as such, once you accept Jesus in your life, you will be made right with God, and His grace and Spirit will be poured into you. So is masturbation a sin? Yes! It is a sexual act done to pleasure yourself. Is oral sex a sin? Yes! It is a sexual act done to pleasure another person. Bottom line, whether you are pleasuring yourself or someone else, it's still a sexual act. Under God's eyes, all sexual act done outside of a marriage means you are sexually immoral.

This subject of lust is a very complicated subject, if I am completely honest with you. You see, every human being has a desire to be sexual. We are like this because God made us this way. However, when you choose to have a relationship with God and to follow Christ, you are choosing to abide by His rules and do things His way. The best part of that is He rewards those who diligently seek him. God says in His word that anything you give up for Him, you will get back ten times in return. So if you give up smoking, sex, or alcohol for God, there is a reward. Whatever you give up to follow Him, He will give you back so much more. I'm living proof of that.

Celibacy while Single

As I stated earlier, I have been celibate for a very long time, and it hasn't been an easy journey. Here's my confession. I can admit that I love Jesus, but I also want to have sex. I can admit that I love Jesus, but I want to pleasure the person I am dating. I can admit that I love Jesus, but I still get horny! I can admit those things boldly because I know they don't define who I am. Please understand that just because you are practicing celibacy, does not mean you don't have any sexual desires or struggle with things like lust.

Personally, I struggled in this area because of things I exposed myself to in the past. Remember I defined *lust* as "living under sexual thoughts." So I began to think about ways I can be free from this place. Being single and dating is extremely fun. I would encourage anyone to date as long as you have boundaries set for yourself. For example, you have got to ask yourself, "Why are you really dating this guy or this girl? Is there a goal or is this just for fun?" Dating while you are single can look like a lot of things to everyone, but the key thing is finding out what it means to you specifically. Being celibate and single was challenging, to say the least. I was celibate because I wanted to do the right thing before God, but I didn't exactly go cold turkey. I didn't have intercourse, but I did perform other sexual acts. I battled with myself for a long time because I knew it was wrong. I knew I was being fake. I claimed I was celibate, but at the same time, I was willing to comprise in a lot of situations with guys. When you are single and celibate, it's a completely different experience than when you are celibate in a relationship. When I was single and dating, I had gotten so good at what I considered self-control with these guys I didn't have an issue going out on dates with. I knew I wasn't going to have sex with them. I knew that if I liked them, I might comprise sometimes; but at the end of the day, I thought I had it under control. I mastered my urges that I was even able to sleep on the same bed with a guy I really liked and not desired to have sex with them. To be honest, if I knew then what I know now, I wouldn't have even put myself in those type of situation that wasn't beneficial to my spiritual growth. Lust and desire can attach itself to anyone. It does not matter what your relationship status is. Whether you are a virgin and dating, single and dating, single and not dating, or whether you are in a relationship practicing celibacy, it can get you!

Being single and celibate in the twenty-first century is extremely hard for both men and women, but it's usually harder for the one who has never practiced celibacy. However, it also doesn't mean it's any easier than the one who is practicing it. I realized I had to stop faking it by having one foot in and one foot out with this celibacy thing. I decided to go cold turkey and be truly celibate. Now with this path I chose, I had no problem attracting men, but I had a hard time keeping them. Most men that I know of are not celibate. I believe they are out there somewhere. If you are reading this and expecting one to find one, I pray God grants you your heart's desire. Now because most men aren't practicing celibacy, trying to get one to commit and understand your journey is tough. But all hope is not lost because if you choose to give up something for the sake of doing right by God, He will reward you. So just be patient and focus on becoming your best self. Now as a woman who is practicing celibacy while single, I believe you will run into a few types of men.

1. There is the guy who is straightforward about his opinions on not having sex and will tell you, "Nah, I'm good" It's a hard pill to swallow, but these are the kind of guys you will eventually learn to appreciate because they were honest with you in the beginning and told you what it was up

front. Trust me, knowing about how they feel about sex beforehand will save you heartache in the future when or if your emotions become involved.

2. Then there is the guy who may seem persistent at first when you tell him you are celibate. Initially, he will be so intrigued because they see you as a "challenge" they can break. Fortunately for you, their true colors will surface. Once they see how serious you are about your walk and commitment, they'll disappear.

3. There is the one who will pretend to be okay with it and actually pursue the relationship with you, but the entire time, they might be living a double life. (I'll discuss this more in my next book, *The Person on the Other Side of the Bed*.)

4. Lastly, there is the guy who will work with you with love, understanding, and respect not only to you, but also to God. This man also values his relationship with God and is able to trust God to lead you. He will not challenge your celibacy but rather be your covering. It also important to note that sometimes God will give you exactly who you need, but it may or may not come in the package you are expecting.

In all four scenarios, only time will be the true test for whatever category you fall into. Again, it's so important to set boundaries for yourself because if you don't, you will look desperate and insecure. Guys can pick that up very quickly. It is also important not to jump into things too quickly because you want to take your time to get to know this person, but that also differs with everyone. There are people who have only known each other for a short time, got married, and have lasting love. Then there are others who have been together for a long time, got married, and ended with a divorce thereafter. These things happen, and it's very situational. Don't compare your relationship experience to what someone else has been through. You should rather pray constantly and ask God to show you who this person is. Again, more details will be in my next book, *The Person on the Other Side of the Bed.* A checklist will be available there before you say, "I do."

When you are single and celibate, the only way to beat lust and things like masturbation and pornography is to figure out where your heart is. Have a heart check as outlined in this book and figure out what your heart truly looks like. Also, keep your mind busy. An idle mind is a devil's workshop! When you have so much free time on your hands, you leave space for the enemy to creep into d your thoughts. While you are single, you should be busy learning about yourself and leveling up in life. Date yourself, work on your credit, travel, get some new hobbies, go to the gym, and, most importantly, always keep God in the center of it all, while you are becoming the person you want to attract. There are too many people who have a checklist or criteria with what that they are looking for in a significant other but aren't even able to bring the same thing to the table, so it's important to work on yourself. Now as I stated before, being horny is not something you can't avoid, but it's possible to keep it at bay. It's all about your perspective. If you are keeping yourself busy, you will find it easier to focus on things that make you happy and are satisfying, even on days when you feel alone and want to be comforted. Now I am aware that in the heat of the moment (i.e., when you are horny), you aren't going to be thinking of reading the Bible or praying. You probably won't want to be as productive because the only thing on your mind is to get a release. Am I right? If you are feeling this way, then I need you to call someone who can hold you accountable. If that doesn't work, then pray—and I mean, seriously pray! If after you've prayed, you still feel the urge to have a release, then that's between you and God. If that happens, you're probably going to feel guilty and down like, "Here we go again!"

I understand because I have been where you are. Before you beat yourself up, remember that the reason that you are failing at this is because your heart isn't right. Until you get that part right with God, it will always be a struggle. I had to do it as well. I struggled for a long time just like you. I had to do a heart check myself after so many times of feeling guilty. I began to take steps to really analyze the area of my life God was missing. What I discovered was that I didn't include God in my financial decision or really anything else in my life. I wasn't paying my tithes for a while. I was making decisions out of pure emotions and fleshly desires. More importantly, I wasn't keeping God at the center of my life. Once I realized this, I prayed to God to ask for mercy and forgiveness first and then I began to make a conscious decision to include Him in my decisions. I decided that no matter how much I thought I need that ten percent, it wasn't mine to begin with. So I had to tithe faithfully. I also read devotionals in the Bible app that dealt with lust. I just decided to include God in my daily activity. It wasn't easy, but it made a difference. Every time I had that feeling, I chose to fight it by giving that energy back to God until I no longer felt the need to masturbate. It was a win. I didn't care if I didn't win every day. I cared that I went from taking losses to gaining several wins until I eventually got delivered. Once my focus changed from pleasing myself to pleasing God, it got better for me. I no longer wanted lust to be the deciding factor of what controls my decisions. Yes, I still get horny, but now my focus has changed from wanting to satisfy my fleshly desires to asking myself if God will get glorified if I gave into it.

That was my heart check and my personal testimony. What would yours be? What would you be required to do? Whatever your heart check is, God must be the center of it all or it won't work. To start the process of your heart check, think about doing the following.

1. Pray and talk to God. Tell Him about your struggles in that area and invite Him into your situation. Tell Him you are sorry and be open and transparent with Him about it.
2. Think about your five senses: sight, smell, taste, touch, and hearing.
3. *Sight.* I need you to dig deep and think about what you have seen throughout your day or even in your past that causes you to lust, then pray about it and invite God in.
4. *Smell.* Think about a *scent* or anything you remember that causes you to sin and pray about it.

5. *Taste.* If it applies, think about what you *tasted* that causes you to be lustful. It could be food or it could a person. Surrender it to God.

6. *Touch.* Think about what you have touched that caused you to be lustful. It could be magazines, sexual partners, or rape. Think deep and pray about it

7. *Hearing.* If it applies, think about what you *heard* and what that sounded like. It could be audio porn, music, etc. Surrender it to God.

In order for you to be free from lust, you must first recognize the source and offer it to God. You must also learn how to shut the gates that makes you to fall. The gates of your soul is what you see, what you hear, what you smell, what you taste, and what you touch. Surrender these senses to God and trust Him to help you control them.

Celibacy in a Relationship

What they don't tell you as a single person is that being single and practicing celibacy is as much as of a struggle as it is in a relationship. As I have stated before, if you are truly celibate, you will run into several types of men. There is the one who will absolutely not be receptive to the idea of no sex before marriage and will eventually disappear, the one who will entertain the idea but eventually stop calling or texting because they realize they can't handle it, and then there's Boaz. Boaz is a man in the Bible who happens to find the love of his life named Ruth. Ruth was a widow who ended up living with her mother-in-law. She was a hardworking woman who caught the attention of a man who ended up becoming her husband. The moral of the story here is to work hard and focus on yourself and, most importantly, on God so He will lead you to the right person. When you have found your Boaz, ladies, you have found your husband, your king, etc. In order for celibacy to work while you are in a relationship, you and your partner have to come to a mutual understanding. If both of you aren't committed to the celibacy path, it will very difficult Be Warned! You both need to have an understanding that the reason you are choosing not to be intimate on that level has everything to do with glorifying God rather pleasing each other. God has to *always* be the primary focus in your relationship. He has to be at the center of the two of you.

I was at a point in my life where materialistic things didn't matter to me anymore. I wanted someone of substance. I had to fine-tune the list to what I thought I really needed in a relationship and a future spouse. I have heard people say against creating a list. Personally, I don't think there is anything wrong with it as long as it lines up with God's will for your life. I believe if you pray for anything according to the will of God over your life, you'll get what you prayed for. But first, you have to ask yourself the motive behind your request. I am a firm believer that God will give you what you need in a partner, and sometimes it may even be what you want. God sees your heart. He knows what you like. He is certainly not going to send you someone you won't be attracted to, but you have to trust Him and not your list. If you want a spouse, then He wants that for you. Sometimes we make a list of materialistic things but not seek God's face. Then we miss out on good people because they didn't check all the boxes on our list.

In a future spouse, I wanted three things specifically: (1) someone who would understand my celibacy journey and is also willing to work with me; (2) someone who will love me for me and is family oriented, and, most importantly; (3) someone whose heart is after God. While writing this book, I was in a relationship with someone I was engaged to. He checked those three major boxes. I was happy then because I actually thought my search was over. I have found *the one*. But he wasn't! Please note, that it is very possible for someone to check all your boxes and still *not* be right for you. I will discuss this further in my next book, *The Person on the Other Side of the Bed*, to explain the importance of having a checklist before you say, "I do."

When I was single, I mentioned earlier that I had mastered the art of dealing with the pressure of not having sex with the guy I was dating that I felt like I was practically invisible. I thought if I could handle being celibate while single, that I can certainly handle being celibate while in a relationships. Well, it was by far the hardest thing he and I had to deal with in our relationship. I mean, it was extremely difficult. Things will get so much harder trying to abstain from sex when you are in a relationship, especially in the godly relationship, because of the biology of your body. There will be plenty of times when you both will get horny and have to figure out how to deal with that issue. Remember, single or not, lust by itself is caused from a heart issue as we discussed in the previous chapter.

Here are some things I suggest you do if you and your partner are struggling in this area. Please understand that these key points should be applied in the context of marriage alone or couples who are celibate for religious purposes. I would be remiss not to point that it's a sin in God's eyes because he doesn't condone it.

1. It's important to understand your partner's sexual history. Why? Unless the both of you are virgins, understanding their history sheds light on how they view sex and the importance of sex in their lives.

2. It is also important to break any soul ties that they have had, whether relationally or generationally. You can do this by digging deeper into the history of their past relationships or learning about their family. A soul tie can be formed it a lot of different ways. There are healthy soul-ties and there are demonic soul-ties. It's up to you to find out what your partner has been involved in. It could be as simple as "anger issues." For example, if you're partner tells you that they had anger issues only after they got out their last relationship, then that's a soul tie that has been carried over that needs to be addressed. It's very important to be open and transparent to one other and seek wise counsel.

3. It is as equally important for you know what triggers the other person sexually and set boundaries. This requires a lot of transparency and open communication with each other. In order for the both of you to win, you have to talk

about these things so the other person understands how to deal with it. It also sheds lights on how to strategically approach situations without coming of as insensitive.

4. Both of you need to take time out to pray together and seek God as a couple. The Bible says, "Where two or three people are gathered, God is present." If you are honestly struggling in this area, go back to the steps I outlined in the book and practice that. Have a heart check and think about what your heart posture looks like. Is pleasing God less important than pleasing each other? Think about it separately then come together and pray on it. There are going to be times when one person will be stronger than the other, but you will not be able to do it by yourself. It will require God's grace. Now I am not saying that you will not have moments of weakness. If you fall, it's okay. Just remember that if are constantly falling, then the problem here is that your heart needs to be checked.

5. It's important to understand each other's love languages. Knowing your love languages can help you understand each other better and get to know what you both need from the relationship emotionally so it can grow.

6. Be practical about what can work for the both of you. Be honest and be open and, more importantly, keep God in the center of your relationship. Do not compare what other people are doing in their relationship with yours. It's important to seek wise counsel, like getting couples therapy, especially in the church to help you navigate it better. Ultimately, what you fill your heart with is what comes back, so make sure that you fill your heart with God's word.

Now I have personally heard about Christian couples practicing celibacy who had different techniques and mechanics they used to keep them focused on being pure throughout the process. I have heard of a couple who didn't kiss at all in their relationships until they were married. I have heard of couples who didn't spend time alone with each other, especially when they went out. I have heard of couples who can't sleep on the same bed. So it's really important to be practical about what would work for you and your partner. Prayer is the *key*! The Bible states that a man must leave his father and mother and cleave to his wife. I am also not here to encourage jumping into marriage because of sex. Marriage is something that should be taken very seriously.

In the Bible, David was a good and wise king who had flaws like everyone else. David committed horrible things like adultery and murder, but God still calls David "His friend." You know why? Because even after all of that, David realized his sin, repented, and asked God to forgive him. God, who loves us unconditionally, forgave him. You see, the Bible describes the life of David as one of trials and tribulations, successes, and failures, just like anyone else. For all his failures, the one thing that didn't change about him was his deep desire to follow God regardless of what obstacles he faced. That's why God called him a man after His own heart. Please don't misunderstand me. I am not condoning adultery or murder at all to any degree. My point is, God will still not count you out if He knows your heart is after Him and repent from your sins. David loved God. He loved obeying God's laws and commands. He did that by mediating on the scriptures. God granted him wisdom and understanding through his daily meditation. So what makes David so unique? His heart! When you sin, lust, or masturbate, do you ever think about why you do it? Do you ever think about how it makes you feel? Are you repentant of your actions to God? When you sin, how does your conscience make you feel? When David sinned, he immediately repented. Do you know what also made a difference? His course of action. David mediated and worshipped in songs (psalms). He made it his duty to pray and seek God's counsel in everything. He was so grounded by the word of God that even when he made a mistake, God refused to look at his mistakes, but rather his heart. That is why God called him His friend.

How does this all tie in? I am here to tell you that your struggle with lust is only as great as you make it seem if you want to be free from it. It's not about how many times you make mistakes or the number of times you slipped up. It's about what you do before and after. The question you need to ask yourself,

"Is the love I have for God more satisfying that my need for sex or the need to be pleasured?" There is a proverb that says your heart is where your treasure is. If all you care about is money, that is where you heart and your mind will be, and that is what God judges you. If

> IS THE LOVE I HAVE FOR GOD MORE SATISFYING THAT MY NEED FOR SEX OR THE NEED TO BE PLEASURED?

your kids and family is where your heart is, they are your treasure. If your mind is constantly filled with lustful thoughts, sex, masturbation, etc., then that is where your heart will be. If you heart and your mind is filled with meditating on God's word and commands, then that will be where you heart is. What I am saying is that it doesn't matter what your actions are, what matters is what you feed your spirit and soul.

If you struggle with lustful thoughts—sex, pornography, masturbation, etc.—and you want to stop, the first thing to do is to make an effort to see what your triggers or causes and then eliminate it. The second thing to do is to pray about it and read your Bible regularly, allowing God to fill you with His word to change you from the inside out. The third thing you need is an accountability partner, someone who you can share your struggles with and will not judge you and someone who can pray with you through it. The last thing you need to do is to understand that changes happen over time. Do not put so much pressure on yourself thinking that you will not do it ever again after the first day. No! Be realistic and create expectations that make sense to you. So if you slip up today and you didn't have one tomorrow, then that is a win. Do not overwhelm yourself. It's not about perfection; it's about progression. Personally, there have been times in my life where I hit a low or when I had done something I knew was wrong that made me feel dirty or unworthy. In those time when I do not know what to say or even how to ask for forgiveness, the prayers below are what helped me get back up.

Prayers

Don't go to bed with another's spouse. Don't think you preserved your virtue simply by staying out of bed. Your heart can be corrupted by lust quicker than your body. Those leering looks you think nobody notices are also corrupt (Matthew 5:28).

Dear God, I thank You for all that You have done for me. I ask that You forgive me for all the wrongs I have done until this point. I understand that You have kept me safe from all harm not because I can control it, but because of Your protection over my life. When it comes to the subject of lust, Lord, I need help. I am human and struggle with self-control. I try so many times to tell myself that I will eventually stop, but it's difficult, Lord. I recognize that there isn't anything that I can possibly do to cause You to love me any more or any less God. In the meantime, I am asking for Your guidance and strength through it all

So I tell you, live by the Spirit. Then you will
not do what you sinful selves want. (Galatians
5:16)

Dear God, Your words says that if I live by the Spirit, then I will not do just anything I want to do, especially when it comes to sex. God, You're going to have to help me on that one because I don't have self-control. When I am single, it's hard. When I am with someone, it's even harder. Please teach me how to submit to Your will and Your ways. I want to do better, Lord, but I just don't know how. Please help me in Jesus' precious name.

Run away from sexual immorality. Every other sin that a person does is outside his body, but those who are sexually immoral sin again their own bodies (1 Corinthians 6:18). You should know that your body is a temple of the Holy Spirit. The Holy spirit is in you.

Dear God, Your word is telling me to run from sexual immorality, but please show me how to do that, especially when I get to urge to do something that I am not supposed to do. I am sorry for the times I have slipped up and made promise to not go down that path, but I can't stop doing this by myself. I need Your help. I need Your grace to see me through. I know now that Your Holy Spirit lives inside of me, and I know You're always watching me too. Please, God, I don't want to continue. I need Your help to change my heart. In Jesus' name, amen.

Don't want her because she is beautiful.
Don't let her capture you with the way she looks.
(Proverbs 6:25)

So God, what You are basically saying to me is You don't want be to only be attracted to someone for how they look. That's going to be tough. I mean I know that looks aren't everything, but You have to help me because I certainly do not want to marry someone I am not attracted to. Help me, Lord, not to lust after this person. Help me to see You in their heart. In Jesus' name, amen!

It's the devil who wants that tempts a person. His own desires lead him away and hold him. This desire causes him to sin. Then the sin grows and bring death. (James 1:14–15)

Lord, Your word states that it is the things in my heart that causes me to sin. It is my desire that leads me away and causes me to sin? Lord, help me and help my heart. I still struggle with lust and sexual thoughts. Please help me and search my heart. Change my heart's posture so I can do right by You. In Jesus' name, amen.

3

Daddy Issues

The term *daddy* issues refers to an informal phrase from the psychological challenges that results from one absent or abnormal relationship with a father. It often evokes a series of emotions that can manifest later on in life and may cause insecurities in relationships. With women, this may cause them to desire paternal figure in the relationship they want to pursue. For men, this may cause their inability to be fathers themselves or have other father-related issues. This definition is true in most cases, but not all.

In a typical American community, there are a lot of fatherless children. This remains an epidemic in our society. "According to the United States Census Bureau, out of 19.7 million children, 1 in 4, live without a father in their home" (National Fatherhood Initiative, "The Proof Is In: Father Absence Harms Children"). Statistics also show that forty percent of children growing up in America today are being raised without their fathers (Wade, Horn, and Busy, "Fathers, Marriage, and Welfare Reform." Hudson Institute Executive Briefing, 1997). According to Young Warriors.org, 75 percent of all adolescent patients in chemical abuse centers come from fatherless home, and 85 percent of all youth sitting in prison today grew up in fatherless homes. It also states that 74 percent of children in the same circumstance are at risk of suffering from emotional neglect, and 165 percent are at greater risk of experiencing notable physical overall. Now as a young mentor myself, I have seen some cases where some youths develop behavioral problems that triggered anger and aggression. Some decide to drop out of high school, become depressed, have low self-esteem and do poorly in school.

Now I want you to stop and really think about what I just said. If you are one of the ones who had an absentee father in your home as a child, be honest and see if any of these describe you. Are you someone who grew up without a father? Then I need you to know that your past does not define who you are. You have got to rise above every statistical barrier. You need to understand that those do not define who you are as a person and who you will be.

Some of you may know the story about a pastor known as Joyce Meyers. At a very early age, she was sexually, mentally, and emotionally abused by her father. It started when she was a very young age and continued as she got older. In one of the articles written about her, she states that her father was a mean, controlling, and manipulative person. He was also unpredictable and unstable. As a result, the atmosphere in their home was filled with fear. The man she was supposed to trust to keep her safe would rape her at least once a week. This caused her to feel shameful, lonely, afraid, unwanted, and unloved. Overall, she was a damaged child. The silver lining she couldn't see at the time was that God always had escape route planned for her life. Sometimes we may go through things in life and often question God, "Why me, Lord?" Sometimes God will take us through the storm instead of taking it away because He has a plan. God always has a plan, even in your worst situation. It was not easy, but Joyce Myers reached a place in her life where she knew she had to forgive her father. Forgiveness is one of the hardest things to do, especially if the person who wronged you is a parent. I need you to remember that forgiveness is not for the other person. It's for yourself. When you forgive the one who hurt you, you are taking your power back from them. When you forgive others, it

> FORGIVENESS IS NOT FOR THE OTHER PERSON. IT'S FOR YOURSELF. WHEN YOU FORGIVE THE ONE WHO HURT YOU, YOU ARE TAKING YOUR POWER BACK FROM THEM

also makes you forgivable in God's eyes. On a YouTube video, Joyce Myers said that God gave her the grace to completely forgive her father. She said that as long as she kept that secret, she wasn't free from it. Can you relate?

I was raised by Nigerian parents. Most older parents were raised on certain traditions and certain cultures. These cultures and traditions are used by most African parents to raise their kids because that's all they know. Unfortunately, these traditions aren't always the best methods, especially if you are raising Nigerian-American children. Generally speaking, my siblings and I were raised by both our parents. My father supported and provided for his family. That's all he knew. As a young adult, I realized that his role as a provider wasn't enough for me anymore. I needed more! My father worked as diplomat. Part of his duties was to travel across the globe, representing his country. My dad always did what he could to provide for his family to live comfortably. As great and financially supportive as my dad was, there was still something he was lacking as a parent. I didn't realize how much his absence would impact my life as a teenager and adult. For most of my life, until my dad retired, I only used to see him about once or twice a year, and every time he was around, we would always argue. Most African fathers aren't raised by their fathers to be affectionate to their children or their spouse. There is a stereotype that it's the woman's job to meet the emotional needs of the children. Because of this, it's hard for fathers to show love to their kids because they don't really know how. Please understand that although providing for your child and having financial stability is important, it's not everything. If you are father reading this book or plan to become one, please understand that you are not weak because you show emotions to your kids. Your kids need to know that you are there for them in every way.

As an adult writing this book, if I had known then what I know now, perhaps my dad and I would have a better father-daughter relationship. But I was young and yearned to build an emotional connection with my dad. Because my dad traveled most of the year, it made our relationship even more estranged when he would come back during holidays. As I grew up, I understood that my dad missed a lot of important moments in my life due to work, and I accepted it. However, what I wanted was for him to see me and understand me for who I am and not the little girl that he used to know. Isn't that what most young adult want from their fathers? When kids grow up in fatherless homes, they can develop a certain form of resentment. If it's not properly addressed as an adult, it can be very detrimental to the person, especially if they are in a relationship. I remember the feelings of hopelessness and a strong dislike for my dad because I felt he couldn't understand me. When I was about twenty-two, I had an emotional conversation with my dad after one of our typical arguments when I expressed to him how I was feeling. I told him my disappointments, regrets, and anger toward him and how he made me feel overall. Nothing really changed after that, but it I realized that I was holding on to some pain because my dad was not as present as I would have liked him to be. I realized that regardless of how I felt about my dad, he is a man who made a choice that unfortunately caused him to be away from his family for most of his career, but he was generally a good father.

For you, that might not be the case. Your father may not have been a provider at all or perhaps he was just a deadbeat. It doesn't change the fact that he wasn't there. You cannot allow his absence to dictate how you should live. Regardless of what happened between you two, you have got to come to the realization that you have to walk away and forgive or find a solution and forgive. Either way, there needs to be a level of forgiveness for you to move forward. Remember that you cannot control what your father did, but you are in control of how it affects you and the decisions you make in your life. Do better for your kids and the next generation. Break the cycle, break the curse.

> YOU CANNOT CONTROL WHAT YOUR FATHER DID, BUT YOU ARE IN CONTROL OF HOW IT AFFECTS YOU AND THE DECISIONS YOU MAKE IN YOUR LIFE

I honestly don't know how my life would have been if I had my dad around like my mom was. Would I have been different? Would his physical presence have an impact on my life or my relationships with men? The truth is, I just don't know. It was at this point that I realized that I have to forgive my dad for his shortcomings and accept him for who he is. Forgiving him gave me a chance to relearn who I was and build a better relationship with him. It took a lot of prayer and self-awareness to get to this point, but this single act of acceptance and forgiveness made our relationship better. I can honestly say with all the love in my heart that my dad and I are in a much better place today.

Now I know that some of you might have the same story. Others may have different stories. You may be in a situation where your father did not want you at all from birth. You might be in another situation where your father was there for a short period but was always in and out of your life. Maybe you just have an estranged relationship with your dad because of how he treated you, your siblings, or your mother? Whatever the cause may be, the bottom line is you have experienced loss from an absent parent. There is a cure for that.

Even though growing up with an absentee father may or may not have played a part on where you are today, there is someone who has always been there with you and for you even when your biological father wasn't, someone who will always have your back no matter what. He will always be here and will never disappoint or fail you because His love is not merited by your actions. There is absolutely nothing you can do to make Him love you any more or any less. You can truly find peace, wholeness, and completion in Him. Who is this person you ask? I'm talking about God the Father. God is not just the Almighty one, He is also your loving Father and your friend. Some of you may ask and say, "If God was such a loving Father, then why did he allow me to go through the pain and anguish like I did? Why wasn't He there to pick me up when I had fallen? Where was this God when I needed help the most?" The answer is, "He was there in the middle of it all." I don't have any answer as to why bad things happen, but I do know God promises to work things out for our good, including the good, the bad, and the ugly. I may not know what your level of pain has been, but I can assure you that once you give it to God and allow Him to fully take over, you will begin to experience true freedom. God will always use that bad situation that you never thought you could escape from and bring out something beautiful from it. Remember that God may not always get you out the situation you are in, but He will always give you the grace to get through it. The scriptures below are words from God's own mouth. If you believe it, say the prayer and you will indeed be free.

Prayers

Though my father and my mother may forsake you, I'll always be there for you Confession. (Psalm 27:10)

Dear God, it is no secret that I have felt abandonment in my past. Because of the burdens, I choose You this day as my freedom. You say in Your word that even though my parents abandon me, You will never to that to me. I ask that You pour Your peace and love on me. I choose today to forgive my parent who abandoned me, I thank You, Lord, that I now know that there is nothing I could do more or less to make You love me more than You already do. I ask You to heal me completely from my hurt, and I trust You now, Lord, because I know that You are always looking out for me.

Can a woman forget the baby she nurses? Can she feel no kindness for the child she gave birth to? Even if she forget her children, *I will not forget you.* (Isaiah 49:15–16)

Dear God, it's amazing to know that even in the worst-case scenario, You will never abandon me. I want to know the type of love You speak off. I know that I cannot go back in time and rewrite history or my past, but I choose this day to give it to You. I ask that You show me and shower me with this unconditional love. I know the love of a woman and her child is great, but Yours is greater. I can only imagine how that must feel. I give You my heart, my mind, and my soul. I receive this love that You have given me in Jesus' name.

> Yes, if you forgive others for the things they do wrong, then your Father in heaven will also forgive you for the things you do wrong. But if you do not forgive the wrong of others, then your Father in heaven will not forgive the wrong things you do. (Matthew 6:14–15)

God, forgiveness of my dad or the ones who have hurt me seems to be a very difficult task to do. There are so many memories, so many events that I cannot seem to forget. Sometimes I don't even know how or if I have the capability of forgiving those who hurt me. I am expressing myself to You today because I need Your help with letting go of this pain. I know I am not perfect, but I've been hurt, Lord. However, in my imperfection, I know I am still going to do wrong. I will need You to forgive me as well. Lord, You are saying that in order for You to forgive me, I have to forgive him. *This is probably the hardest thing that I ever had to do, but I'm ready to let go of this pain. I forgive my dad for the pain that he caused in my life, for not being present, and for not having my back when I needed him. I forgive myself for holding on to this for so long. I ask that You envelope me and cover me with this unspeakable love You offer. Take it away, Lord. I give it to You, Lord, so I can be healed and forgiven. In Jesus' name, Amen!*

- "I am going to do something new. It is already happening. Don't you recognize it? I will clear a way in the desert. I will make rivers on dry land" (Isaiah 43:19 GW).
- "God is not a man that he should lie, nor a human being, that he should change his mind. Has he said, and he will not do it? Or has he spoken, and will not make it happen" (Numbers 23:19 NET).

Lord, You are doing new things in my life. Making a road in the desert and finding rivers in the driest of land is logically impossible to the human mind, but they are Your words so I choose to believe it. What You are saying sounds impossible, but obviously it's possible for You because You are not a human being that You should lie. I choose this day to believe that You are doing something new in life. I'm holding on to Your every word because You don't lie. Just as You make roads on deserts and rivers in dry land, I believe I am a walking miracle, free from that which has held me bound. I thank You, Lord, for starting something new in me. I thank You, Lord, that You stay true to Your word and keep Your promises. In my moments of doubt or setback, keep me grounded and continue to remind me that You have already set me free because of Your Son, Jesus. In Jesus' name, amen!

Love is patient and kind. Love is not jealous, it does not brag, and it is not proud. Love is not rude, is not selfish, and does not become angry easily. Love does not remember wrong done against it. Love takes no pleasure in evil, but rejoices over the truth. Love patiently accepts all things. It always trust, always hopes, and always continues strong. (1 Corinthians 13:4–7)

Dear God, Your definition of what love is may sound foolish to some, but not to You because that is how You love and expect us to love others. As I am only human, I don't think I can selflessly love others on my own. If I rely on Your strength, I can do it. Lord, in in times of difficulty, when I don't have the strength, teach me how to love others with patience and be kind to others even if I feel they don't deserve it. Help me not to be jealous or want what someone else have. When my blessings start pouring in, keep me humble and help me not brag or be too proud. Help me not to be rude to others or take pride in evil. Help me not to become easily angered by things beyond my control. I want to accept and trust You in moments of weakness and doubts and to stay in You when I have no more strength to give. Teach me, Lord, how to give unconditional love. This is pray in Jesus's name, amen!

4

Hello, Fear

Wikipedia describes *fear* as "an unpleasant emotions caused by the belief that someone or something is dangerous and can likely cause pain or threat." Merriam-Webster dictionary describes it as "an unpleasant, often strong emotion caused by the anticipation or awareness of danger." Being afraid can stop you from moving forward or progressing in life. Fear causes you think that there is something wrong with you. If you aren't careful, it will have you thinking that you will never make it in life. You have to learn to overcome that which scares you.

It is the fear of being alone that causes people to jump from one relationship to the next. It is the fear of not being accepted that causes people to commit suicide. It is the fear of wanting to be liked by everyone that causes depression and sadness. It is the fear of rejection that causes people not to accomplish their hope and their dreams. These are just to name a few things that fear does.

Here are a few of my favorite quotes on fear.

1. "You gain strength, courage, and confidence by every experience in which you really stop to look fear in the face. You are able to say to yourself, 'I've lived through this horror. I can take the next thing that comes along'" (Eleanor Roosevelt).

2. "I've learned that fear limits you and your vision. It serves as blinders to what may just be a few steps down the road for you. The journey is valuable, but believing in your talents, your abilities, and your self-worth can empower you to walk down an even brighter path. Transforming fear into freedom" (Soledad O'Brien).

3. "Remember your dreams and fight for them. You must know what you want in life. There is just one thing that makes your dream become impossible: the fear of failure" (Paul Coelho).

Everyone is afraid of something. I want you to really think about it. What scares you in life? Close your eyes just for a moment and think about what terrifies you the most about your life. I can almost guess that whatever you fear has been holding you back and held you captive for a long time, hasn't it?

Now I need you to see yourself in your mind being free from this fear. It's okay if you cannot visualize it yet, but you have got to come to a place of awareness to be able to recognize this fear and find practical ways to overcome it. First, you must have an understanding where fear comes from. Fear comes from Satan. Wherever he is, that's where fear is. God, on the other hand, is love. Wherever God is, there is no fear because God's love is perfect. To really overcome any fear in your life, you have to understand God's love. Secondly, in order to get rid of a fear, there has to be a level of hope. You also have to understand that you cannot be afraid of something and claim you have faith. Faith and fear do not go together. I want you to think of a time in your life when you were at a very low place. Think back to what you saw and experienced and then think about where you are now. I can say for a fact that one of the things that kept you going is hope. Being hopeful is a powerful tool that you can use to trick your mind into believing that you can rise up from the bottom. When people are hopeful, they are wishing for their situation to be better. Sometimes hope triggers certain actions that allows you to be in a much better place. Hope and faith in God go hand in hand. The Bible defines *faith* as "the substance of things hoped for, the evidence of things not seen" (Hebrews 11:1). Have you ever prayed about something that even though you haven't seen it, you know God has done it? Have you ever applied for to a job that even though you haven't gotten a callback for an interview, you prayed and believed that you got it? That's what faith is. Faith and hope in God go hand in hand. You can't say that you have one and not the other. However, the opposite of faith is fear! You cannot claim to have faith in God to supply all your needs and still act like He won't provide. You cannot claim to have faith in God to heal you of your broken heart when the words you speak over your life are contradictory.

For a very long time, I never understood the word *fear* outside the standard definition of "being afraid." It wasn't until a few months into this chapter that God began to teach me on how to deal with fear indefinitely. As I was thinking about fear, I came up with an acronym to change your perception and how to apply it in your life. Fear means to:

Face
Every
Area of
Restriction.

Everyone has different kind of fears: insects, snakes, heights, etc. The fear that I am referring to is something that cripples you at the thought of it. It's something that keeps you hostage in your mind, something that can affect and destroy your purpose. From today onward, I would like to challenge you to change your perception of fear. I want you to see it as an opportunity rather than an opposition. Fear is something that Satan uses to trick people into being trapped for the rest of their lives. You must fight him back.

I define fear as an opportunity to "face every area of restriction" (FEAR). Once you start to treat FEAR like a challenge and not an obstacle, your entire world perspective will change. In time, you will learn to master it. When you are scared of something, instead of cowering down, you must learn to question that part of you that's scared and face it head on. It was the fear of driving that caused me not buy a car or drive any car for a long time. In fact, I wish I had known how to master fear at that point in my life. I'm sure there would have been a great deal of things that I would have done confidently without being afraid. Before I purchased my first car, I obtained my license for years. When people asked me why I wasn't driving, I would make an excuse as to why I wasn't. I have some amazing friends and family members who would willingly take me anywhere I wanted, so I never really thought of it as an issue.

For years, I caught the bus back and forth to work because I was so scared to drive. I tricked myself into believing that I didn't need a car, but the reality was I was just afraid. I realized that the fear of driving started years ago when I was a teenager. On several occasions, I would have this this nightmare. I would see myself getting into a car to drive, but either it wouldn't start or wouldn't move. Sometimes I would see myself in the car literally stuck with no sense of direction. I would wake up in fear. I cannot count the number of times I had the same dream, but it happened for years. It wasn't until I purchased my first car that I shared the story with my mother. Because of this recurring dream, I didn't want to drive. Every time I would be given an opportunity to drive, my heart literally felt like it was about to fall out my chest. Not only was I nervous, I was terrified of the dreams coming true. As of today, I am beyond grateful to say that not only did God provide the funds for me to get a car, but I can also say that I am one of the best drivers that I know of. LOL! Some of my friends might disagree because they think I'm a speed racer, but no one can truly understand the joy and freedom I feel when I drive. That's mostly because I decided to turn my fear from opposition to a challenge that I wanted to win.

FEAR (facing every area of restriction) causes freedom when you challenge that which scares you. We can agree that most people can say they are afraid of something, right? The most common thing that scare people is the fear of the unknown: not knowing what the future holds, if you will ever accomplish your dreams, if you will ever get married, if you will ever pass a test, if you will ever have enough money to pay your bills, or if you will ever get the career of your choice. Now in order to fight every area of restriction in your life, the first thing you have to do is to pray about it and then fight and face it. For me, at some point in my life, I got tired of asking people to give me rides. I got tired of the public transportations and depending on people. The only choice I had was to get into a car no matter what. The only way I could beat this fear of driving is if I practiced. There is a famous proverb that says "Practice makes perfect," but what I've come to learn is that if the presence of the unknown causes you to be afraid. The only way you can change that is if you put into practice of what scares you and then allow God to teach you how to trust Him by surrendering. For example, the only way I mastered the fear of driving is only because I practiced how to drive and I became great at it over time. I gained so much confidence until that horrible dream became thing in the past. Fear will have you crippled so bad that it will cause you to miss your destiny and purpose if you don't recognize it.

I was up praying one night and studying the word as usual when I had a vision—or perhaps it was a dream, I'm not quite sure. I saw myself sitting on the floor in a dark room. I looked frightened. As I sat there, I saw a hand appear under the door that I didn't see at first. I got up to see where the mysterious hand was coming from. As I got up to open the door, I saw a figure of a man. I couldn't really see his face. All I was able to see what a bright light and a hand. In that moment, I knew that God had visited me. As I began to look away from the light, I heard Him speak to me, saying, *Will you let me in? I cannot come in unless you let me!* So I let him in. Then He said, *You have to give it to me.* At first, I didn't understand what He was talking about. In that moment, the only thing that came to my mind was *rejection.* He was telling me that I have to give it to Him so He can heal me and set me free from it.

You see, for a very long time, while I was celibate and single, I met several guys. When I explained to them what my standpoint was regarding waiting until marriage to have sex, I didn't expect them to completely understand where I was coming from. Some saw it as a challenge but would eventually give up on me altogether. Their responses to me over the course of the years made me realize that it was a form of rejection. These men made me feel like I wasn't worthy enough, that there was something wrong with me just because I was saving myself for marriage. Thus the cycle continued. With each guy who disappeared or stopped talking to me, I realized it sowed a seed of rejection and built a wall up that was surrounded by fear. I began to fear anyone getting close to me, not trusting God to come through for me.

While I was having this vision, He made me realize that and He was telling me to give it to Him. I started to cry, thinking about all the pain and disappointments I had gone through. He was there telling me to give it to him so I can receive complete healing. I saw a big gold key in His hand. He told me, *If you want to be free, you have to unlock the door.* I grabbed the key and tried to unlock the door, but it was stuck. I couldn't unlock it so I said, "Lord, why would you give me this key if it doesn't work?" He walked up behind me and whispered softly, *Because you need me.* He then proceeded to place His hand over my hand. Before we turned the key, He said, *I am the key to your freedom. I have already set you free and healed you from this place. I will continue to do so, but you have to continue to invite me in for you cannot do this on your own. You have found a helper in me.* With His hand over mine, we turned the key together. Instantly, the walls came down. I woke up and realized what had happened. God was showing me that I was already free form rejection and fear. All I needed was to invite him.

Sometimes fear will have you so crippled and paralyzed and that even when you have an opportunity to be free from what are afraid of, you will have a hard time accepting it because you are now in familiar territory that brings you comfort. Most people enjoy what is convenient. They will rather stick to and deal with things that are familiar to them even though it's a bad situation. It's the same reason why a woman will stay in a relationship even if she is being physically or verbally abused. The fear and the idea to start over with someone else and date again is terrifying, so she'll stay and say things like, "The devil you know is better than the one you don't." This is a complete lie from Satan himself. Satan, the enemy, is the father of lies. The Bible says that he has come to steal, kill, and destroy. He is roaming the earth, seeking who to devour. He is wicked and evil. You have to be aware of the devices and things he will use to lure you into a trap. If he can't lure you into fearing something mentally, then he will lure you in fearing something physically. If he can't attack your body, he will attack your emotions.

Those insecurities you have didn't come just from anywhere. Those thoughts about suicide didn't just happen randomly. That fear of the unknown and the fear of dying didn't just happen overnight. It came from somewhere. It came from your enemy Satan. If you let him in, if you do not fight and face all your areas of restriction, you will lose the battle. You cannot afford that because God has given you all the tools you need to win. So then what do you do? How do you overcome the fearful you versus the one who is still scared but wants to fight? You have to find out the root of your fear. Finding out why you are afraid will give you a deeper understanding on how to address it. God said in His word that He has not given you the spirit of fear, but of power, love, and a sound mind. Therefore, if you find yourself feeling scared, you must counteract that fear and fight it because it didn't come from God. You must also dig deeper and find out exactly how God feels about fear. Remember who you are to him and speak those truths over your life. You need God's help.

If you are wondering how God feels about you, read below (https://activechristianity.org/a-letter-of-love-from-god-to-you).

My Child,

- *You may not know me, but I know everything about you. (Psalm 139:1)*
- *Yes, know when you sit down and when you rise up. (Psalm 139:2)*
- *I am very well in the know with all your ways. (Psalm 139:3)*
- *I know and can number all the hairs on your head. (Matthew 10:29–31)*
- *I made you to look like me (Genesis 1:27).*
- *In me you live and move and have your being. (Acts 17:28)*
- *You are my offspring and you come from me. (Acts 17:28)*

- *I knew you even before your mother met your father. (Jeremiah 1:4–5)*
- *I chose you always and forever. (Ephesians 1:11–12)*
- *You were not a mistake, for all your days are written in my book. (Psalm 139:15–16)*
- *I determined the exact time of your birth and where you would live. (Acts 17:26)*
- *You are fearfully and wonderfully made. (Psalm 139:14)*
- *I knit you together in your mother's womb. (Psalm 139:13)*
- *And brought you forth on the day you were born. (Psalm 71:6)*
- *I have been misrepresented by those who don't know me. (John 8:41–44).*
- *I am not distant and angry, but am the complete expression of love. (1 John 4:16)*
- *And it is my desire to lavish my love on you. (1 John 3:1)*
- *Simply because you are my child and I am your Father. (1 John 3:1)*
- *I offer you more than your earthly father ever could. (Matthew 7:11)*
- *For I am the perfect Father. (Matthew 5:48)*
- *Every good gift that you receive comes from my hand. (James 1:17)*
- *For I am your provider, and I meet all your needs. (Matthew 6:31–33)*
- *My plan for your future has always been filled with hope. (Jeremiah 29:11)*
- *Because I love you with an everlasting love. (Jeremiah 31:3)*
- *My thoughts toward you are countless as the sand on the seashore. (Psalm 139:17–18)*
- *And I rejoice over you with singing. (Zephaniah 3:17)*
- *I will never stop doing good to you. (Jeremiah 32:40)*
- *For you are my treasured possession. (Exodus 19:5)*
- *I desire to establish you with all my heart and all my soul. (Jeremiah 32:41)*
- *And I want to show you great and marvelous things. (Jeremiah 33:3)*

- *If you seek me with all your heart, you will find me. (Deuteronomy 4:29)*
- *Delight in me and I will give you the desires of your heart. (Psalm 37:4)*
- *For it is I who gave you those desires. (Philippians 2:13)*
- *I am able to do more for you than you could possibly imagine. (Ephesians 3:20)*
- *For I am your greatest encourager. (2 Thessalonians 2:16-17)*
- *I am also the Father who comforts you in all your troubles. (2 Corinthians 1:3–4)*
- *When you are brokenhearted, I am close to you. (Psalm 34:18)*
- *As a shepherd carries a lamb, I have carried you close to my heart. (Isaiah 40:11)*
- *One day, I will wipe away every tear from your eyes. (Revelation 21:3–4)*
- *And I'll take away all the pain you have suffered on this earth. (Revelation 21:3–4)*
- *I am your Father, and I love you even as I love my Son, Jesus. (John 17:23)*
- *For in Jesus, my love for you is revealed. (John 17:26)*
- *He is the exact representation of my being. (Hebrews 1:3)*
- *He came to demonstrate that I am for you, not against you. (Romans 8:31)*
- *And to tell you that I am not counting your sins. (2 Corinthians 5:18–19)*
- *Jesus died so that you and I could be reconciled. (2 Corinthians 5:18–19)*
- *His death was the ultimate expression of my love for you. (1 John 4:10)*
- *I gave up everything I loved that I might gain your love. (Romans 8:31–32)*
- *If you receive the gift of my Son Jesus, you receive me. (1 John 2:23)*
- *And nothing will ever separate you from my love again. (Romans 8:38–39)*
- *Come home, and I'll throw the biggest party heaven has ever seen. (Luke 15:7)*

- *I have always been Father and will always be Father. (Ephesians 3:14–15)*
- *My question is ... Will you be my child? (John 1:12–13)*
- *I am waiting for you. (Luke 15:11–32)*

Love, Your Dad.
Almighty God

So now we pray, we fight, and we win. So then my question to you is, what are you truly afraid of and how bad is it? Please understand that fear and God don't mix. To God, fear is obsolete. It cannot be found. So as you pray the prayer below, I hope that you will be free and delivered from the spirit of fear. These prayers have helped me overcome the restriction that has kept me bound.

For God has not given you the spirit that
makes you afraid. He has given you the power of
the spirit, love, and self-control (2 Timothy 1:7).

Dear God, Your words states that You have not given me the spirit of fear, but. Lord, I still have a lot of fear—fear of abandonment, fear of rejection, and fear of not being loved properly. I do not want to feel these things any longer, so please take them away from me. Shower me with Your spirit. Show me love and teach me how to practice self-control, amen.

Do not be anxious about anything, but pray
and ask God for everything that you need. When
you pray, give thanks. (Philippians 4:6)

Dear God, You just said that I shouldn't be anxious for anything, but I have to admit that it's really hard for me not to. Things keep happening that causes me stress. When I get stressed, I become so worried. I am asking that You help me depend on You more each day. I thank You for what You have done for me so far and what You are going to do. I give

You thanks as Your words states. Lord, in my moments of anxiety and worry, please help me remember that You are in charge.

I leave you peace, my peace I give you. I do not give it to you as the world does. So don't let your hearts be troubled. Don't be afraid. (John 14:27)

God, Your words state that my heart should not be troubled because you have given me peace? There is so much that goes on in my mind on a daily basis, I am tired. I think about my future and how I am going to reach my goals, I think about past hurts and pains. I am angry, Lord. I have allowed my anger to fester for a while. Forgive me, Lord, if I had sinned while angry. I am asking that You give me this peace that You speak of. Peace to preserve, peace to understand, peace to be calm, and peace to know what You have everything under control. In Jesus' name, amen.

The Lord saves those who fear Him. His angels encamp around them. (Psalm 34:7)

Heavenly Father, You save those who fear You and have Your angels encamp around them. Please, Lord, encamp your angel around me today. I don't want to be afraid of the world. I am asking that You turn whatever doubt, fear, or worry that presents itself in my life and make me whole. Even as I go from day to day, please protect me and guide me always on how to keep trusting You in the process. In Jesus' name, amen!

I say this because I know what I have planned for you. I have good plans for you. I don't plan to hurt you. I plan to give you hope and good future. (Jeremiah 29:11)

Dear God, the fear of the unknown is a really big thing for me. I am at a point in my life that I am not as confident as to what my future looks like. I struggle daily, living paycheck to paycheck. I would like to be in a position where I am debt free, able to save the way I want to and having financial freedom. There is so much going on in my thoughts that sometimes I do not know how I am going to make it through. Help me to remember Your word that regardless of what I am experiencing right now, You have good plans for me, plans to give me hope and a good future. Help me remember that when I became anxious or scared. Help to me stay focused on the path that I am currently at. I am asking that You continue to guide my path into that good future in Jesus' name.

Listen, I gave you power to walk on snakes
and scorpions. I gave you more power than the
enemy. (Luke 10:19)

Thank You, God, for showing me that regardless of what I am going through, I am still able to speak life into my situation. Your word gives me more power than the enemy, right? Since I have that authority from You. I speak and declare that today I will move forward and not backward. I speak life into any negative situation that presents itself. I speak peace in my mind, my thoughts, and my spirit. I speak and take authority over anything against my life. I will not continue to live in fear because You have given me the power the overcome. I decree and declare that from now on, I will win mentally, emotionally, financially, spiritually, and relationally. In Jesus' name, Amen.

5

Friendships

The Power of Friendships

Everyone who ever said they don't need a friend are all liars. Is that you? Have you ever made that type of statement to yourself or others? The way I see it, everyone needs a friend. It may not be a lot of friends, but everyone needs someone they can talk to about things of any sort. I looked up the definition of *friendship* online, and Wikipedia states, "A friendship is a relationship of mutual affection between people. It's a stronger form of interpersonal bond an association."

Personally, I have always said life is better when you have a friend you can rely on. I want to speak on why friendships are important to have.

A. The power of friendship reduces health problems that is a product of loneliness. Being lonely is something that can happen when you feel rejected or perhaps when you don't know anyone supporting you in any way. The thought of not having a proper support system can cause series of mental disorders, like paranoia, insomnia, etc., just to name a few. It is very important to surround yourself with people who will always be there for you, such as your family members. Good and loyal friends are hard to come by, so if you have a few good ones, make sure you hold on to them. Just remember to move cautiously.

B. If you choose to date, it's important to build on a friendship first. When you are friends with someone you are interested in dating, it results to the best kind of relationships. In my previous relationships, this is something that I wish I had done more of. I think I was just carried away with the way I felt for this person and went with the flow, rather than taking my time to build on something foundational. It's very important to not just be in relationship with someone, but you should also spend time with them. I believe that if a couple establish friendship first, it will certainly help progress the relationship.

C. The more loyal friends you have, the less stressed you become. There is nothing like having a village. There is a saying that states, "It takes a village to raise a child." So if it takes a village to raise a child, don't you think it will possibly take a village to hold an adult man or woman accountable? It is important to surround yourself with people who will be a blessing to you. It provides a space for trust and, most importantly, accountability.

D. The power of friendship is important because you cannot do everything by yourself. There is another quote that says, "There is no *I* in team." It is important to connect yourself with people who can get you to your desired goal faster. These types of friends are called "destiny helpers." They come into your life specifically to help you carry out the vision and purpose God has placed in your life. But it is very important to tell the difference between *destiny helpers* and *destiny snatchers*. Destiny snatchers will come like wolves in sheep clothing, so it's important to move prayerfully and cautiously among the people you allow in your circle.

E. The power of having friendships will trigger empathy, the ability to understand and share the feelings of another. When you have a friend who is going through something, you will empathize with them if you are a good friend. You will put yourself in their shoes so you can get a much better understanding on how to respond.

Friendships are important to have because you are able to gain another perspective. For example, if you are doing something wrong, a good friend will be able to point that out and tell you. Sometimes we get so wrapped up in our present circumstance that we are incapable of being objective until someone else points it out.

Like-Minded People

I cannot stress the importance of surrounding yourself with like-minded people. People in your circle should continue to make you grow, evolve, and generally make you better. For as long as I could remember, I was never lacking friends, but I was always cautious who I allowed myself to trust. As women, God wired us to have intuition, an innate feeling or knowledge that something isn't right with any given situation. A lot of times, we ignore our intuition to give the other person the benefit of the doubt, but the thing about your intuition is that it never fails you. If your heart is telling you that something or someone isn't right for you, do not ignore it. Do not paint the red flags white. I never had a hard time making friends, but I have always found it difficult to let people in with good reasons based on past experiences. I always had people in my circle who were envious of me. I wasn't able to see it at first because the thought of accepting that someone in my circle who was not truly happy for me was sickening. I'm the type of person who always desired her friends to win. If I win, then they win as well. I have always been the one to carry people and want them to be the better version of themselves. But after a major heartbreak with a man I thought I was going to marry, I decided to level up—I'll talk about this more in my next book, *The Person on the Other Side of the Bed*. Knowing the type of people you keep in your circle is very important to where you go, I had to learn that regardless of how much I want to help others, everyone is on their own personal journey. Secondly, not everyone is able to go where you're going. The sooner you start to realize that, the better your mindset will become.

If you are the smartest one out of your friends, then you need better friends. Through my personal experiences, I have come to realize three truths about the type of friends you need in your life:

1. You need a friend who is doing better than you in life, is doing what you want to do, and who can help you get to their level. You need someone you could consider a mentor.
2. You need someone who is on the same level as you, someone who is running the same race as you and who you can talk to and bounce ideas off. You need someone who has the same drive and passions as you, helping and motivating each other to be better.
3. You need a friend who you can pour into, someone who looks up to you but also someone you can make better, and desires to be like you.

BEFORE YOU BECOME A LEADER, YOU HAVE GOT TO LEARN HOW TO SERVE OTHERS

All leaders have someone they admire. Before you become a leader, you have got to learn how to serve others. Now I need you to think about the three types of friends mentioned above and examine your circle or your relationships. As you begin to do so, ask yourself, "What is the purpose of this friendship? Am I growing, evolving, and becoming a better person because of this relationship? How has my life significantly improved since they came into my life?" You have to ask yourself these questions because you do not want to be connected to the wrong people. You do not need people in your life who are users and take from you without giving back anything. That doesn't mean that you should only make friends with people who can do something for you first in order to form a friendship with them, but rather try to figure out the benefit of that friendship for the both of you. If you decided to be friends, you have to figure out the place that you are at the time and see if allowing this person into your life is beneficial for both of you. This applies in both friendships and relationships. If you don' take your time to analyze each friendship, you will become frustrated and exhausted at some point, especially if it's not going the way you had hoped. Learn to pick and choose your friends wisely because building important relationships is important to your success. Even God knew Adam could not do everything on his own so He created a "helpmate" for him. The term *helpmate* doesn't only apply when it comes to relationship but also to friendships. Any friendship that is not making you better and adding productivity to your life needs to but cut off immediately.

Comparison Is a Killer

Whether you are doing right or wrong, there is always going to be someone who will have something to say. You should never live your life to please others and make someone else happy. One thing that I would like you to understand is that you are unique. God made no mistake when He created you. You have a unique DNA that no one on this planet has. Because of that, you have got to appreciate your difference in friendships. Everyone has a different path in life. When you compare yourself to someone, it's very dangerous. The only comparisons I would consider healthy should be to those that inspire you to make changes in your life for the better. This goes back to the different kinds of friendships I had talked about earlier.

As an individual, before you decide to get into any type of rela-tionships or friendship. It is so important to know and understand who you are as a person. I cannot stress that enough. When you know yourself and who you are as a person, you will never allow someone else to define who you are. Even when they do, you will have the power to change the narrative of the story. I have also been the type not to have as many close girlfriends. As a teenager, I found myself becoming friends with girls that were in a duo group. Things happen that causes them to fall out and then others come into my life. I have always had a hard time trusting people in general. When it came to friendships, that is something I was always cautious of, these are things that you need to look out for because they do exist. The truth is, the higher you level up in life, the more hate you are going to receive. There are people who are going to be happy for you but also others who don't want you to succeed unless they are succeeding first, so be very careful.

In the society we live in today, it is extremely hard not to compare yourself to people because of social media. For example, if you have been single wanting to be in a relationship or marriage, it can be hard to see other couples' "relationship goals" on Facebook or Instagram without you feeling or wanting that or saying to yourself, "I wish that were me." Maybe there is an opportunity or job that you and someone else applied for, and they end up getting the job rather than you. It is very well possible that it will create a level of rejection and comparison. *Why them and not me?* I have already touched on the topic of rejection, but it's always safe to say that if you ever had to compare yourself to anyone, the underlying cause might be coming from rejection that needs to be addressed first.

Everything in life is all about timing. God has a great purpose for your life and has given you the tools you will need to accomplish everything with your abilities and talents. These gifts are what you should be focused on in your life right now. Remember that you are on God's timetable. If someone is getting married, that's their timeline to get married, not yours. If someone has kids, that's their timeline. If you want to have kids, yours will come! If someone is at a position that you want to be in, that's their timeline. Yours will come! You have got to think of life as being in competition with yourself. You are on your personal journey, making moves and decision for yourself and not for others. When you start to see yourself as a man or woman with a race to win, it will immediately change your perception and how you look at things. There are a lot of instances that you may not even compare yourself to others, but there are things that people will do to show you that they are very envious and jealous of you. Most of the time the jealously is very subtle, but if you pay attention and move cautiously, you will be able to see it. The Bible states in Philippians 2:3 (NLT), "Do not be selfish; don't try to impress others. Be humble, thinking of others as better than yourselves."

Let me remind you again that you are God's masterpiece. He made no mistakes creating you. Remember that you can be anything but you cannot possibly be everything at once. You are not God. If someone else is going after something that they want to do for themselves, that doesn't mean you have to do it too. Rather, find out what your purpose is and ask God to direct your path. It's okay for you or someone else to win. Comparing yourself to someone else will definitely make you feel miserable and unhappy. There is only one thing that you can do in life that costs absolutely nothing, and that is being you. It costs nothing! Do not think that you have to dim your light to make anyone else shine. Do not think that you have to change who you are to please someone. Faking it to make it will not take you very far. For one, you can only pretend for so long until the real you comes out, and you will look like a counterfeit. Pretending to be someone that you are not takes too much thinking and planning so why do any of that? Just live your truth. When you stop comparing yourself to others, you start being better at what really matters to you. Play your own game and not somebody else. The prayer below will help you in the times when or if you are dealing with the art of comparison and you need a breakthrough.

> **WHEN YOU STOP COMPARING YOURSELF TO OTHERS, YOU START BEING BETTER AT WHAT REALLY MATTERS TO YOU.**

Some friends may ruin you, but a real friend
will be more loyal to you. (Proverbs 18:24)

Dear heavenly Father, there is no way I could know the intentions of the people that are in my circle and the people that I am about to meet. Please give me keep from any friendship that may ruin me. I ask that You expose any hidden agendas of anyone in my life and remove them from my life completely.

Do not be deceived: "Bad company ruins
good character." (1 Corinthians 15:33)

Dear God, please help me not to surround myself around bad company. I want to move cautiously. I have certain friends who do certain things that I don't agree with, but I don't want to stop being friends with them. I am asking that You guide my path and move them completely from my life in Jesus' name.

Keep your lives free form the love of money
and be satisfied with what you have. (Hebrews
13:5)

Dear God, You know times are difficult right now so it's kind of hard to keep from the love of money and the fulfillment that it gives. You know, Lord, that we need money for pretty much everything, but I am asking to keep me from being greedy. I don't want to focus just on money that it pushes me to do things I wouldn't want to do. Help me, Lord, to be content and satisfied with where I am now, knowing that all things will work together for my good at the end of the day.

Iron sharpens iron, and one man sharpens
another. (Proverbs 27:17)

Dear God, Your word says, "Iron sharpens iron." Please look at my life at connect me with like-minded people who I can sharpen, and vice versa. Surround me with people who are after Your heart and destiny helpers that can take me to my next level. I no longer want to be the big fish in a little pond. I no longer want to be the only one that pours in my friends, Lord. I would like to be connected with people who we can pour into each other. Help me, Lord. In Christ's name, I pray.

Whoever works with the wise becomes wise,
but the companion of fools will suffer harm.
(Proverbs 13:20)

Dear Lord, You are basically telling me to show me my friends so people can see who I am. I admit that I have not been really good at picking friends. To be honest, I am kind of a people pleaser. I want other people to like me. I am not sure if it's because of some insecurities that I have. Anyway, I definitely do like to hang out with a bunch of fools because I do not want people thinking that I am foolish. So please give me some friends who give me wisdom so I can have a better selection of friends. In Jesus' name, amen!

"I say this because I know what I have planned for you," says the Lord. "I have good plans for you. I don't plan to hurt you. I plan to give you hope and a good future." (Jerimiah 29:11)

Dear God, I thank You for what You said in your word that my whole life is planned, plans not to hurt me but give me a good future. I really like to believe this Lord. It is very hard sometimes to see good things happening for others and not me. Sometimes I wonder when my time will come. I often get annoyed and frustrated because I feel like I have been waiting for a while. I am not in any means trying to rush You, but I am just asking that You continue to give me the daily strength and faith that is needed to keep trusting in Your word. I decree and declare that I will receive that good future You have planned for me. Help me, Lord, not to compare myself to others and remind me that my timeline and my life plan is in Your hands alone. In Jesus' name, amen!

Trust in the Lord with all of your heart. Do not depend on your own understanding. Remember the Lord in everything that you do and he will give you success. (Proverbs 3:5–6)

A person may think of plans but the Lord decides what he will do. (Proverbs 16:9)

Dear God, I thank You for always speaking to me even when I am not listening. Your words says to trust You with all of my heart and to not depend on my own understanding. Once again, Lord, I'll need Your help to do so. You know how I am wired. You know that I am a perfectionist and I overanalyze. Sometimes when things don't go according to plan, I get upset and frustrated. I don't get any peace until I have got it figured out. I also understand that acting like that showcases as if I am in control of what plays out in life, but really You are in charge of my life. I am asking You today, Lord, that You be in the driver's seat and GPS of my life. Your word basically states it doesn't matter how well I plan, You will obviously have the final say. So today, Lord, I yield and submit to Your plans and Your ways. When I make plans for my life and my future, help me not to move based on my own understanding and remind me to surrender it to You first before making any decisions. In Jesus' name, amen!

He should not compare himself to others.
Each person should judge his own actions. Then
he can be proud of what he has done himself.
Each person must be responsible for himself.
(Galatians 6:4–5)

God, help me, Lord, not to compare myself to others. I need Your help navigating life and my purpose and calling. Sometimes it is hard not to compare myself to others because of how things are moving quicker for them than it is with me. I, however, don't want to compare because I know everything has its own timing and its own season. As I reflect on what You have done for me up until now, I thank You, Lord, for where I am been and my progress. I am still alive so that means You still have more for me to do. Lead me on Your path so I can continue to be proud of all my accomplishment. Help me, Lord, to keep my eyes fixed on You.

Do you think I am trying to make people
accept me? No, God is the One I am trying to
please. Am I trying to please men? If I wanted to
please men, I would not be a servant of Christ.
(Galatians 1:10)

Dear God, I don't want to live my life to please others. I want to please You. Forgive me for all actions done so far than have proved otherwise. I want to live my life acknowledging You in everything that I do. Help me remember that You are the only one that matters. Your opinions and thoughts are the only one that counts. I no longer want to live my life based on the barometer and standards of someone else. Teach me how to solely be dependent on You in all the areas of my life.

The thing you should want most is God's
kingdom and doing what God wants. Then all these
other things will be given to you. (Matthew 6:33)

God, sometimes it is very hard to seek You first, especially it's not a routine for me however, my ultimate goal is seek You first in everything that I do, but I know I don't always do that. Sometimes I get caught up in other things that are obviously not as significant to You. I understand now that putting You first should be top my priority. I ask that You help me do that. In Jesus' name, amen.

6

New Beginnings

As I mentioned in my introduction, I was inspired to write this book based on the experiences I have encountered growing up in the church. I realize that there are a lot of silent struggles that our youths and young people deal with, especially if they are Christians trying to live their lives for God. I wanted to create a platform for things that I struggled with in my life as a Christian. I wanted to share some of those experiences in hopes that the reader will see themselves in my stories, suggesting practical tools and prayer that you can use and say to overcome those struggles.

As you read each prayer point and story, I do not want you to just be done with the book. If you are seeking deliverance and guidance, it has to be done with a consistent mindset. If you struggle in any area that I mentioned in these chapters, I encourage to pray those points daily. You must have an understanding that the closer you are to God, the closer He is drawn to you. It's not about perfection but progression. The more you continue to put Him first, the more He will give you things that you need. Remember, it's not about how many times you tried to break your bad habit. It's about what is in your heart. True change comes from your heart. You have already won the battle as God is on your side. Invite Him in to your life. Most importantly, tell Him to change your heart posture so you can start to experience true freedom in Him.

God is in love with you. He doesn't care about what you have done. You are still redeemable. Once you ask Him to come into your life and confess your sins, truly repentant of your ways, He will forgive you and give you a clean slate to start over. He loves you that much. If you are convicted to accept Christ into your heart and are ready to accept Him, please say the prayer below.

> For God so loved the world that He gave His only begotten Son, that whoever believes in him may not be lost but have eternal life.(John 3:16)

God, I thank You for this moment. I thank You for making me realize that I have been living my life in a way that doesn't please you. I choose You today to be the Lord of my life. I confess that I am a sinner. I believe in my heart that You sent Jesus to die for all of my sins and my struggles. I surrender now to Your will and repent of all of my sins. Help me to keep my eyes focused on You as I start this new path and guide me daily through the process of pleasing You and living for You. Remove anything that is not from You. I am inviting You to take Your rightful place in my life. In Jesus name' I pray, amen!

You have just taken the first step to be part of God's family. God loves you more than you can comprehend. There is nothing you can do to make Him love you any more than He already does. The Bible says that once you pray for the repentance of your sins and accept Jesus to be in your life, there is joy in heaven. The angels are celebrating you today for making these steps. You have officially solidified your position in heaven. Congratulations! Now go be great and live out your best life in Christ Jesus!

About the Author

Milola Charles is an upcoming fashion entrepreneur, a writer, and the author of the new book, *Me Versus Me*. With a decade of life experiences, Milola has an unfiltered, compassionate, and unique voice that is geared toward the youth and young adults. She has experience with organizing single women's group meetings to brainstorm on the challenges they face with their godly walk in their singleness. She teaches practical scriptural ways of dealing and overcoming those challenges. Milola always had a passion for writing and helping people, which motivated her to write her first book to help Christian youths and singles who are struggling silently in their walk with God.

Milola lives in Baltimore, Maryland. She is a Coppin State University alumni who majored in health management and business management. She works at the Maryland Department of the Environment in connection with the Environmental Protection Agency (EPA).

She is the second of four kids, and she enjoys spending time with family and friends.

Facebook: Milola Charles
Instagram: @iammilola

CPSIA information can be obtained
at www.ICGtesting.com
Printed in the USA
LVHW070004180222
711184LV00010BA/740